MODEL RAILWAY
PROJECTS

MODEL RAILWAY PROJECTS

by
R.A. PENFOLD

BERNARD BABANI (publishing) LTD
THE GRAMPIANS
SHEPHERDS BUSH ROAD
LONDON W6 7NF
ENGLAND

PLEASE NOTE

Although every care has been taken with the production of this book to ensure that any projects, designs, modifications and/or programs etc. contained herewith, operate in a correct and safe manner and also that any components specified are normally available in Great Britain, the Publishers do not accept responsibility in any way for the failure, including fault in design, of any project, design, modification or program to work correctly or to cause damage to any other equipment that it may be connected to or used in conjunction with, or in respect of any other damage or injury that may be so caused, nor do the Publishers accept responsibility in any way for the failure to obtain specified components.

Notice is also given that if equipment that is still under warranty is modified in any way or used or connected with home-built equipment then that warranty may be void.

© 1981 BERNARD BABANI (publishing) LTD
First Published — September 1981
Reprinted — February 1989
Reprinted — December 1991

British Library Cataloguing in Publication Data
Penfold, R. A.
  Model railway projects
  1. Railroads — Models — Electronic equipment
  I. Title,
  625. 1'9'028   TF197

  ISBN 0 85934 070 8

Printed and bound in Great Britain by Cox & Wyman Ltd, Reading

PREFACE

Model railways have, of course, been very popular for very many years now, both with adults and children. Electronic projects for use with model railways are a relatively recent development, but the range of projects and the ingenuity of the more complex ones has rapidly increased to the point where it is now possible to produce layouts having a high degree of realism and sophistication. There are even microprocessor based model railway projects, although these go beyond the scope of this publication.

The main aim of this book is to provide a number of useful but reasonably simple projects for the model railway enthusiast. The projects covered include such things as controllers, signals and sound effects units and to help simplify construction stripboard layouts are provided for each project.

WARNING

Please note some of the projects included in this book are
powered from the mains.

Always be sure to observe all the usual safety precautions
including correctly earthing the equipment and not working
on equipment when it is still connected to the mains supply.

CONTENTS

	Page
CHAPTER 1. MODEL TRAIN CONTROLLERS	1
Constant Voltage Controller	6
The Circuit	7
Components	10
Construction	11
Improved Starting	13
Components	15
Construction	15
Simple Pulsed Controller	15
Components	21
Construction	22
Improved Pulsed Controller	24
Components	28
Construction	29
Inertia/Breaking Controller	29
Components	34
Construction	35
Pulser	39
Components	43
Construction	44
CHAPTER 2. ACCESSORIES	47
Point Controller	47
The Circuit	48
Components	51
Construction	52
Additional Outputs	52
Automatic Signal	52
The Circuit	56
Components	58
Construction	59
Signal Controller	61
The Circuit	62
Components	64
Construction	65
Electronic Steam Whistle	67
The Circuit	68

Components. 71
Construction 72
Two Tone Horn 73
   The Circuit. 73
   Components. 77
   Construction 78
Simple Train Chuffer 80
   The Circuit. 80
   Components. 83
   Construction 84
Automatic Chuffer 84
   The Circuit. 87
   Components. 89
   Construction 90
Amplifier. 92
   The Circuit. 92
   Components. 94
   Construction 94

Semiconductor leadout and pinout details 96

CHAPTER 1

MODEL TRAIN CONTROLLERS

The complexity of train controllers varies considerably from one design to another, but in general the level of performance is reflected in the cost and sophistication of the controller. The most simple types normally use an arrangement of the type shown in Figure 1 or Figure 2.

If we take Figure 1 first, this merely consists of a step-down transformer to reduce the mains voltage to the appropriate level, and also to give isolation from the mains for safety reasons, a bridge rectifier to convert the alternating current (AC) from the transformer to a direct current (DC), and a variable resistor (or rheostat as it is sometimes known) to vary the power fed to the motor.

The rectifier is essential because the electric motors employed in normal model engines will only operate from a DC supply, and simply switch rapidly between forward and reverse movement if fed from AC supply so that no progress is made in one direction or the other. As will be apparent from this, the direction of the motor (and the train) depends upon the polarity of the supply, and the direction of the train can be controlled by altering the polarity of the output. This is the purpose of the switch at the output. The supply fed to the train is not a steady DC supply since the circuit does not include any smoothing components. This does not matter though, as DC motors run perfectly well from a pulsating supply.

The overload protection device is included to protect the circuit against an excessive output current flow in the event of an accidental short circuit across the output, or some other form of overload (such as a jammed motor which can have a very high current consumption). There are several methods of overload protection, and a common one is to use a special thermistor. This is a device which normally has a very low resistance, and therefore has little affect on the circuit. If it passes a high current it heats up, and this rise in temperature has the effect of causing a considerable increase in the resistance of

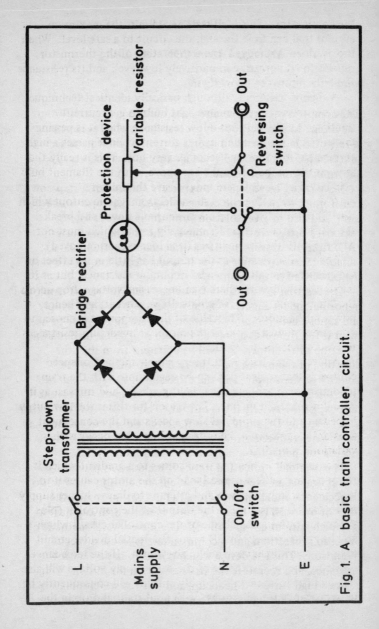

Fig. 1. A basic train controller circuit.

the component. This high resistance limits the maximum current that can flow through the circuit to a safe level. When the overload is removed, the temperature of the thermistor returns to its normal, comparitively low level, and its resistance similarly returns to a low figure.

A slightly different, although basically identical technique, is to use an ordinary filament light bulb to give current limiting. A light bulb has a low resistance when it is passing low currents, and a much higher current when it passes a high current and the filament becomes very hot. This is really the same as the method described as above, with the filament bulb being used as a simple and inexpensive thermistor.

A third technique is to use an electromagnetic cutout which is triggered if an excessive output current flows, and breaks the output circuit until it is manually reset (which must not be done until the overload has been located and removed).

The variable resistor at the output has little or no effect on the circuit when it is at or near minimum resistance, but as its resistance is increased there is an increasing voltage drop across the component, giving reduced voltage, current, and hence power in the motor. The value of the component is chosen to give a low enough power in the motor at maximum resistance to ensure that the train does not move.

A severe drawback of this very simple method of speed control is that it gives poor speed regulation, with the train tending to stall as it climbs a slight gradient, and run fast as it goes down a slight incline. The reason for this is the low output impedance of the supply at slow speeds and the consequent substantial changes in the output voltage that occur with variations in loading.

For example, when the train comes to a gradient which it starts to climb, the increased load on the motor causes it to have a reduced impedance and attempt to draw a higher supply current. The resistance at the output of the controller (plus the innate output impedance of the controller circuit which will be comparitively small) forms a potential divider circuit together with the impedance of the motor. If the impedance of the motor falls, its share of the total supply voltage will also fall, and the increase in its supply current will consequently be only marginal. Furthermore, with a substantial drop in the voltage fed to the motor, and a small increase in the supply current, it is likely that the power fed to the motor will actually fall. With the train trying to climb a gradient it is increased power that is needed, not a reduction in power, and the train therefore slows down and probably stalls.

The reverse occurs when the train runs down a gradient, with the load on the motor reducing and its impedance increasing as it tries to draw less current. The increased impedance results in the share of the total supply voltage appearing across the motor increasing, and motor current only reduces very slightly. The power fed to the motor may actually increase since there is only a small reduction in the motor current and a fairly substantial increase in the voltage fed to the motor. The increased power in the motor and the fact that the train is going down a gradient combine to produce a very large increase in speed.

There is an allied effect which makes it practically impossible to produce a realistic start, with the train tending to suddenly shoot off at high speed. This is due to the fact that the motor has a very low impedance when stationary, and a much higher impedance when it is operating. This results in very little voltage being developed across the motor while it is stationary until the variable resistor is at almost minimum resistance, and as a result there is not enough power developed in the motor to start the train until the variable resistor is at virtually minimum resistance.

When the motor does start its impedance rises accordingly, giving reduced supply current but also a greatly increased voltage across the motor. This results in a sudden jump in the power fed to the motor which causes the train to move off at quite high speed.

In the circuit of Figure 2 there is no need for a reversing switch as the variable resistor (or potentiometer as it should be called in this case as all three terminals are connected) controls both the speed and direction of the train. The circuit is much the same as that of Figure 1, but the mains transformer has a centre tap and gives double the output voltage when compared to that used in Figure 1.

With the slider of VR1 at the centre of its track there will be exactly the same potential at the slider as appears at the centre

4

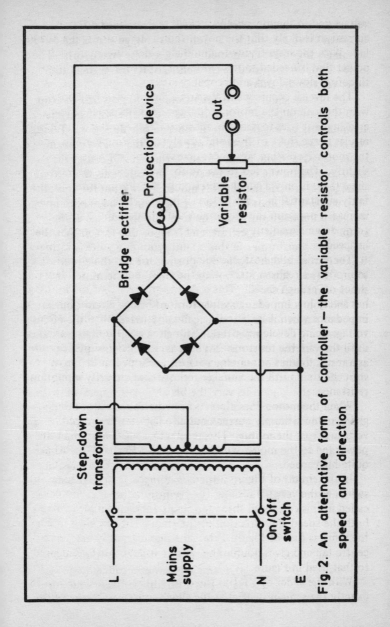

Fig. 2. An alternative form of controller – the variable resistor controls both speed and direction

tap of the mains transformer. There is no voltage difference between these two points, and thus no voltage across the output terminals which are connected between these two points. The potentiometer is ajusted to the centre of its travel then, in order to stop the train.

Moving the slider of the potentiometer up towards the top end of its track takes this point positive of the other output terminal and causes the train to move in one direction. Taking the slider down towards the lower end of the track takes the slider negative of the other output terminal, and causes the train to move in the other direction. In both cases the output voltage increases as the slider is moved away from the central stop position, as does the speed of the train. The maximum output potential is only half the total supply voltage at the output of the rectifier circuit, and it is for this reason that the step-down transformer in this circuit requires a voltage rating which is double that of the transformer used in the circuit of Figure 1 (and double the voltage required by the motor at maximum speed).

This controller uses a simple form of bridge circuit, but in terms of performance it is not really any better than the circuit of Figure 1. This configuration still gives a fairly high resistance in series with the motor at low speeds, giving consequent poor speed regulation and starting performance. It is possible to produce a simple electronic version of these circuits, where a potentiometer is used to vary the bias fed to a transistor, with the latter operating like a high power variable resistor in conjunction with the potentiometer. This has the advantage of not needing a special high power variable resistance, which is necessary with the circuits of Figure 1 and Figure 2 due to the high dissipation in this component at most speed settings, but the circuit still has a high output impedance at slow speeds with the consequent disadvantages this brings.

Constant Voltage Controller

A reasonably simple type of controller that gives improved starting and low speed performance is the so called "constant voltage" type. This is really just a variable voltage regulator circuit which in theory controls the speed of the motor by controlling its supply voltage, with no variations in the supply voltage occuring due to variations in loading of the motor and supply. Many supplies of this type provide far from perfect regulation, but even if the output impedance is not zero, it is usually still quite low and supplies of this type usually give good results in practice, even at low speeds.

The reason for the comparatively high level of performance is quite simple; due to the low output impedance of the controller the motor is able to draw increased supply current when climbing a gradient without any really significant fall in the supply voltage. Similarly, when the train runs down a slope and the motor draws less current, the supply voltage still remains virtually constant. The motor is thus able to draw more or less power as circumstances dictate, and good speed regulation results.

Improved starting performance is also obtained. When stationary the motor consumes quite a high current and power as the speed control is advanced, due to the low impedance of the motor. This high power results in the motor starting before the speed control becomes well advanced. When the train does start, the impedance of the motor falls giving a consequent reduction in the power consumed by the motor, and this also helps to prevent the train shooting off at high speed. However, results obtained with this type of controller are not perfect, and a certain amount of skill and practice may be needed in order to obtain really realistic starting. But, with this type of controller it is at least possible to obtain realistic starting, which is not the case with the most simple types of controller.

The Circuit

Figure 3 shows the circuit diagram of a simple but very effective constant voltage train controller. This uses an integrated circuit voltage regulator (IC1) to give high performance coupled with a simple and quite inexpensive circuit.

T1 is the mains transformer which steps-down the mains voltage to the appropriate level and isolates the rest of the unit from the dangerous mains supply. No on/off switch is shown, and is not really necessary if the unit will be disconnected from the mains when not in use, but one can of course be added if preferred.

7

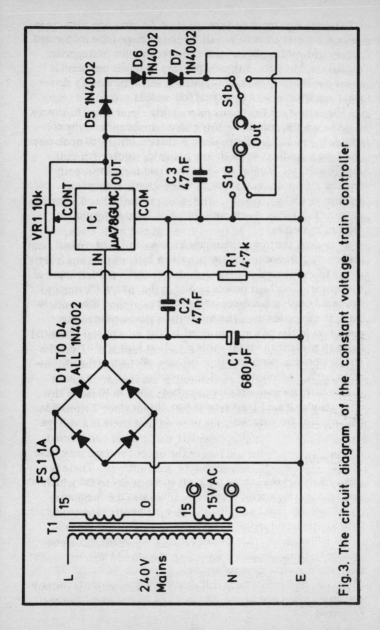

Fig.3. The circuit diagram of the constant voltage train controller

8

There are two secondary winding on T1, and one of these is connected direct to two output terminals to provide a 15 volt AC output for accessories such as electric points and signals. This supply could alternatively be used to power a second controller circuit if desired. The other secondary of T1 drives a bridge rectifier formed by D1 to D4, and C1 provides a reasonable amount of smoothing to give a fairly ripple free DC supply. As mentioned earlier, DC electric motors run perfectly well from an unsmoothed supply, but in this case it is still necessary to include a smoothing capacitor since the regulator circuit does need a smoothed supply in order to function properly!

IC1 is quite a complex device, but its basic action is to stabilise the voltage at the control (cont) terminal at 5 volts by means of a negative feedback network from the output. If the slider of VR1 is set to the right hand end of its track, the control terminal is connected direct to the output terminal, and with the control terminal stabilised at 5 volts the output is set at the same potential. If the slider is moved to the left there is a potential divider action across the section of VR1's track to the right of the slider, and the left hand section of the track plus R1. This gives a voltage drop from the output to the control terminal, and the output has to go to a higher potential in order to maintain 5 volts at the control terminal. Thus the further VR1's slider is taken to the left, the higher the output voltage becomes, reaching a theoretical maximum of a little over 15 volts with the slider fully to the left. In practice this voltage will not be maintained at full output since T1 provides an insufficient voltage (bearing in mind that there is a voltage drop of about 1.5 volts through IC1 under these conditions), and due to component tolerances the output voltage may have a maximum figure of only about 14 volts anyway. There is a voltage drop of about 1.5 to 2 volts through D5 to D7 which are included in series with the output, and so the maximum output voltage could be as low as about 12 volts. However, any normal model train should work well from a smoothed supply of 12 volts or so. The maximum continuous current available from the unit is 1 amp, and this should also be sufficient for any normal model train.

The reason for including D5 to D7 in series with the output is simply to give a lower minimum output potential from the

unit. Perhaps a little suprisingly, 5 volts was not found to be
sufficient to operate any of the author's model engines even
with no rolling stock in tow. It was almost sufficient though,
and would possible be enough to operate some model engines.
It was therefore thought advisable to have a somewhat lower
minimum output voltage and the rectifiers were added at the
output for this purpose. The nominal minimum output
potential is slightly in excess of 3 volts. If preferred, D5 to D7
can be replaced by shorting leads to give an increase of about
2 volts in the maximum and minimum voltages of the unit.

S1 is the forward/reverse switch, and C2 and C3 are decoupling capacitors that are needed to prevent IC1 from
becoming unstable. IC1 incorporates output current limiting
circuitry which protects the circuit against overloads, and
further protection is given by the inclusion of fuse FS1.

Components: Constant Voltage Controller (Figure 3)

Resistor
R1   4.7k 1/3 watt 5%

Potentiometer
VR1   10k 1in carbon

Capacitors
C1   680μF 25V
C2   47nF ceramic plate
C3   47nF ceramic plate

Semiconductors
IC1   μA78GU1C (1 amp four terminal regulator)
D1 to D7   1N4002 (7 off)

Switch
S1   DPDT toggle switch

Transformer
T1   Standard mains primary, two 15 volts secondaries
            each having a current rating of 1 amp or more

Miscellaneous
Case of adequate dimensions
0.1in matrix stripboard panel
20mm 1 amp quick-blow fuse and 20mm chassis mounting
fuseholder

10

Control knob
Output sockets
Mains lead, wire, solder, etc.

Construction

The circuit must be housed in a case which has a screw-on lid
or cover so that the mains wiring is not easily exposed. The use
of a metal case is recommended as this can then act as a heatsink for IC1, which has to dissipate several watts under certain
operating conditions, and therefore needs a fairly substantial
heatsink.

Figure 4 gives details of the 0.1in matrix stripboard component panel and wiring of the controller. Start by cutting out
a board having 18 strips by 17 holes using a hacksaw (the
board is not sold in this size), and then drill the two 3.3mm
diameter mounting holes which are for 6BA or M3 fixings.
There are no breaks in any of the copper strips and so the
components can then be soldered into position on the board,
making quite sure that C1 and the rectifiers are connected with
the correct polarity. Also be careful not to leave out the single
link wire.

When the component panel has been completed, check
carefully for accidental short circuits between copper strips due
to small blobs of excess solder, and then wire the board to the
rest of the unit and complete all the point to point style wiring.
The mains earth lead is connected to the case via a soldertag on
one of the mounting bolts of T1. In the interests of safety it is
essential that the case is properly earthed to the mains earth
lead. IC1 can be bolted to the case to give it the necessary
heatsinking, but it will probably be necessary to use a small
aluminium bracket to help fix it to the case. It is not essential
to use an insulation kit to insulate IC1 from the case since IC1's
heat-tab and the case both connect to the negative supply rail.

Probably the most convenient type of output socket for the
unit is either wander sockets, or some form of terminal post.
However, you can of course use any type of socket you like
provided it is a kind that is capable of handling currents of up
to an amp or so without problems.

Before switching on the finished unit and trying it out in

11

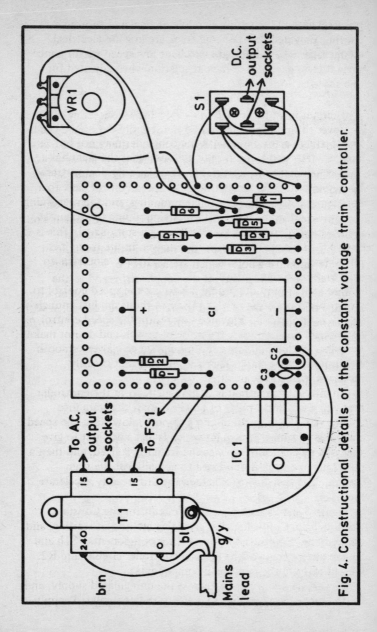

Fig. 4. Constructional details of the constant voltage train controller.

12

practice, give all the wiring a couple of final and thorough checks. Provided the train and track are in good electrical contact, the unit should give excellent low speed performance since it gives excellent voltage regulation when adjusted for low speeds.

Improved Starting

The starting performance with the controller may not be exceptionally good, and it may be found that the train has a distinct reluctance to start. This effect is easily demonstrated by running the train fast, turning the speed control back to a position that gives slow but reliable running, and then returning the speed control to this position after stopping the train. It is almost certain that the train will remain stationary! This is not really a fault in the controller, or even in the train, it is just a fact that mechanisms of this type have a reluctance to start due to various factors.

One way around the problem is to use the speed control to give a very short burst of high power to the train, just enough to jerk it into action. Provided you return the speed control to the right position after the pulse of power, and do not make the pulse too long in duration, this should give a very smooth and quite realistic start. This is something that is easily mastered with a little practice.

An alternative method is to have a circuit in the controller that will give a short pulse of power to spur the train into action. Thus in order to obtain a smooth, slow start, the speed control is advanced to a point which is just sufficient to give slow but reliable running once the train has started, and then a push button switch is depressed to actually get the train started. The speed control is then used to steadily accelerate the train.

Figure 5 shows a simple add-on circuit for the Constant Voltage Train Controller that gives this method of starting, and this only requires the addition of three components. S1b and D7 are components of the original controller circuit, and R2, C4 and PB1 are the additional components.

R2 and C4 are connected across the unregulated supply, and C4 therefore rapidly charges via R2 to the unregulated supply

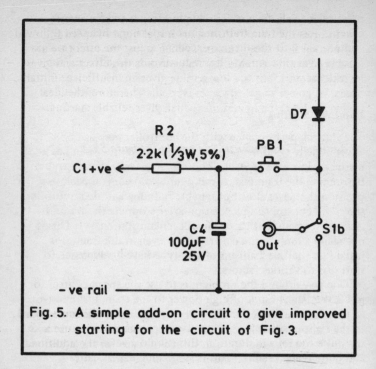

Fig. 5. A simple add-on circuit to give improved starting for the circuit of Fig. 3.

voltage (which is about 23 volts under no load conditions). If PB1 is operated, C4 is connected to the motor via the forward/reverse switch S1, and it rapidly discharges into the motor to give the required short burst of high power that spurs the train into action. R2 prevents a significant current from flowing direct from the unregulated supply to the output, and ensures that only a short pulse is produced at the output no matter how long PB1 is depressed. When PB1 is released, C4 rapidly charges through R2 so that it is ready for the next operation. D7 blocks the output of C4 from the output circuitry of IC1, and ensures that the additional circuitry does not damage the regulator circuitry.

The specified value for C4 is that which gives best results with the author's layout and locomotives. However, you can experiment with the value of this component and may find that a slightly higher or lower value gives slightly better results.

Too high a value is not desirable as it tends to give an effect that causes the train to do a short initial burst of speed followed by normal slow speed running, which is just the effect we are trying to avoid! A fairly low value avoids this effect and gives a realistic start, but too low a value gives an insufficient initial burst of power to get the train started. Therefore, the ideal value for C4 is the lowest one which gives reliable starting.

Additional Components: Add-on Unit (Figure 5)

Resistor
R2   2.2k 1/3 watt 5%

Capacitor
C4   100μF 25V

Switch
PB1   Push button to make release to break type

Construction

The additional circuitry can be incorporated on the same board as the main controller circuitry, but it is necessary to use a board six holes wider in order to make space for the additional components on the left hand side of the board. This modification is shown in Figure 6.

Simple Pulsed Controller

Better low speed and starting performance can be obtained using a pulsed controller where the signal fed to the motor is not a straight forward variable DC potential, but is a series of pulses with the average potential being varied to control the speed of the motor. Ideally the voltage pulses should be of reasonably high amplitude so that each pulse gives plenty of power in the motor. At slow speeds the train is then driven by a series of strong pulses that resist any tendency to stall, or to run fast out of proper control down hills.

Figure 7 shows the circuit diagram of a simple Pulsed Train Controller which is similar in operation to an ordinary mains lamp dimmer circuit. However, this circuit operates at a low

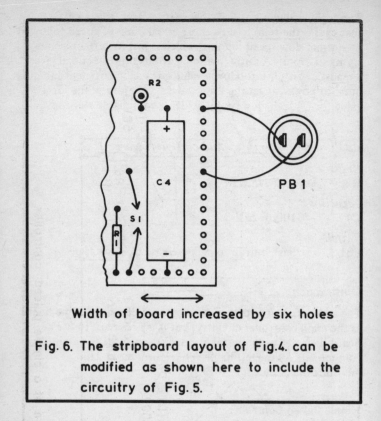

Width of board increased by six holes

Fig. 6. The stripboard layout of Fig.4. can be
modified as shown here to include the
circuitry of Fig. 5.

voltage with T1 being used to step-down the mains voltage to
the required level of 15 volts, and this also isolates the circuitry
from the mains so that there is no danger of an electric shock
being obtained if anyone touches the output terminals or any
of the other wiring to the right of T1. As in the previous
design, there are twin secondaries on the mains transformer
with one being used to power the controller circuitry, and the
other providing a 15 volt AC output. As both the controller
circuitry and the train's motor require a DC supply, D1 to D4
are used as a bridge rectifier which fullwave rectifies one output of T1 to give a pulsating DC supply. Note that no smoothing
is provided, and this is not merely a matter of smoothing not

16

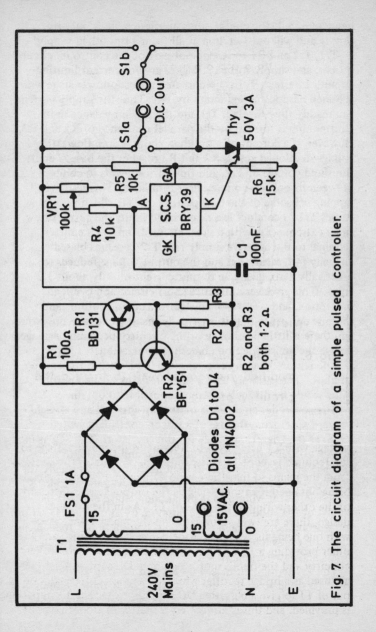

Fig. 7 The circuit diagram of a simple pulsed controller.

17

being required: the circuit relies on there being a pulsating supply and will not function at all from a smoothed supply!

Tr1, Tr2 and R1 to R3 are not part of the controller circuit proper, and simply form a straight forward current limiting circuit. In effect, Tr1 is used as an emitter follower stage which is biased hard into conduction by R1. Thus the supply current can readily flow through Tr1 and the low impedance in its emitter circuit formed by the parallel resistance of R2 and R3. However, if a current of more than about 1 amp flows, the voltage developed across R2 and R3 reaches the base – emitter threshold voltage of Tr2, and this device begins to conduct between its collector and emitter terminals. This results in Tr2 tapping off some of the base current of Tr1, which in turn causes Tr1 to conduct less heavily and limits the current flow. In an extreme case with a short circuit from Tr2's emitter terminal to the negative supply rail, Tr2 becomes biased virtually into saturation and the output voltage reduces to practically zero, giving an output current of only about 1.2 amps. This gives very effective short circuit and overload protection, and is superior to electromagnetic cutouts and thermal devices in that it is virtually instantaneous in operation, and there is little possibility of the circuitry becoming damaged before the limiting action comes into operation.

The reason for using two resistors in parallel in the emitter circuit of Tr1 is simply that a single resistor of the appropriate value would be difficult or even impossible to obtain.

The controller circuitry is quite conventional and straight forward apart from the use of a silicon controlled switch (SCS) as the triggering device for the thyristor. The SCS is used in a sort of relaxation oscillator circuit, and the GK terminal is not needed when the device is used in this way. Normally the SCS does not conduct between its anode (A) and cathode (K) terminals, but it will do so if the anode voltage exceeds the voltage at the anode gate (GA) terminal by about half a volt or so. Furthermore, once in the state of conduction it remains in this state for as long as a significant current flows between the anode and gate terminals.

The GA terminal is biased by R5 and R6, and the anode terminal is fed from the supply via the C – R timing circuit formed by VR1, R4 and C1. The voltage at the GA terminal is a little over half the supply voltage, regardless of what the supply voltage happens to be at any instant. The situation is very different at the anode terminal which is initially at zero voltage since C1 will be in an uncharged state. As the supply voltage starts to rise at the beginning of each half cycle, the voltage at the anode rises as well, but lags behind the supply voltage due to the delaying effect of the C — R network.

With VR1 at minimum resistance there is very little phase lag, and in consequence the anode voltage very quickly goes above the GA terminal by a sufficiently large amount to trigger the SCS. This results in C1 being discharged into the gate of thyristor Thy1 by way of the SCS, and this pulse of current is sufficient to trigger the thyristor into conduction. Like an SCS, once triggered a thyristor continues to conduct until the current flow through it falls to a low level. In this case the current drops to zero at the end of each half cycle when the supply voltage becomes zero. Thus the thyristor switches on early in each half cycle, and continues to conduct until the end of that half cycle.

Figure 8(a) shows the waveform across the supply rails, and Figure 8(b) shows the output waveform of the controller with VR1 at minimum resistance. There is obviously somewhat less than full power at the output because the initial part of each half cycle has been cut out by the action of the circuit. There is also a small voltage drop through the thyristor. However, both these factors only cause a marginal power loss, and for practical purposes there is full output power when VR1 is set at minimum resistance.

If VR1 is set for somewhat higher resistance there is a significant lag between the anode voltage and the supply voltage, and the anode voltage will not be high enough to trigger the SCS until about half way through each half cycle. This gives the output waveform shown in Figure 8(c), and obviously represents about half output power.

Adjusting VR1 for about maximum resistance results in a considerable lag between the anode and supply voltages, so that it is not until very late in each half cycle that the anode voltage reaches the trigger level and the thyristor is triggered. This gives an output waveform of the type shown in Figure 8(d), and there is obviously very little power fed to the load.

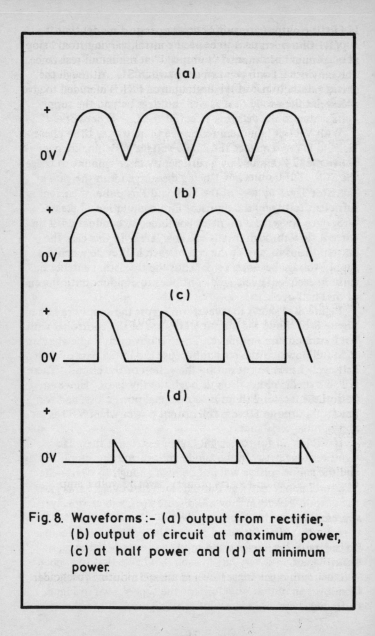

Fig. 8. Waveforms :- (a) output from rectifier,
(b) output of circuit at maximum power,
(c) at half power and (d) at minimum
power.

20

In fact the output is insufficient to operate a model train.

VR1 thus operates as the speed control, varying from "stop" at maximum resistance to "full speed" at minimum resistance. The only other control is reversing switch S1. Although the circuit has built-in current limiting, fuse FS1 is included to give added protection.

Components: Simple Pulsed Controller (Figure 7)

Resistors, all ½ watt 5%

R1	100 ohms
R2	1.2 ohms
R3	1.2 ohms
R4	10k
R5	10k
R6	15k

Potentiometer

VR1	100k lin carbon

Capacitor

C1	100nF plastic foil (type C280)

Semiconductors

SCS	BRY39
Tr1	BD131
Tr2	BFY51
D1 to D4	1N4002 (4 off)
Thy1	3 amp 50 volt thyristor

Switch

S1	DPDT toggle switch

Transformer

T1	Standard mains primary, twin 15 volt 1 amp secondaries

Miscellaneous

Case
0.1in matrix stripboard panel
Control knob
20mm 1 amp quick-blow fuse and chassis mouting fuseholder to suit
Output sockets

Mains lead, wire, solder, etc.

Construction

The unit is constructed along the same lines as the previous project, and Figure 9 gives details of the component panel and wiring of the unit. The component panel is based on a 0.1in matrix stripboard having 16 strips by 14 holes, and there are no breaks in the copper strips.

The thyristor is not mounted on the component panel, but is either mounted on the rear panel of the case or on a mounting bracket. A component having a TO—66 encapsulation is used in the prototype controller, but any type having a current rating of about 3 amps and a voltage rating of 50 volts or more should be perfectly suitable. The TO—66 case of the component is also its anode terminal, and the connection to this is made via a soldertag on one of the mounting bolts. An insulating kit must be used when mounting the thyristor so that its case (and anode) are insulated from the cabinet which connects to the negative supply rail. No harm will come to the unit if this insulation should fail since there will simply be a short circuit across the anode and cathode of the thyristor, effectively bypassing the controller circuitry and giving full output power continuously. One advantage of pulse type controllers is that there is very little power dissipated in the output device since it is either switched hard on, or fully off, and is only in an intermediate state during brief transitions. When switched off it consumes no significant power since only minute leakage currents flow. When switched on there is a high current passing through the device, but there is very little voltage developed across it with most of the supply voltage appearing across the load. In either case there is very little power developed in the device and the thyristor in this design does not require a heatsink.

One slight problem with controllers of this type is that a certain amount of radio frequency interference is generated. This is due to the fast risetime of the output waveform and the consequent harmonics of the 50 Hertz mains frequency that are produced. While it is possible to include suppression components to filter out the higher frequency harmonics, only

22

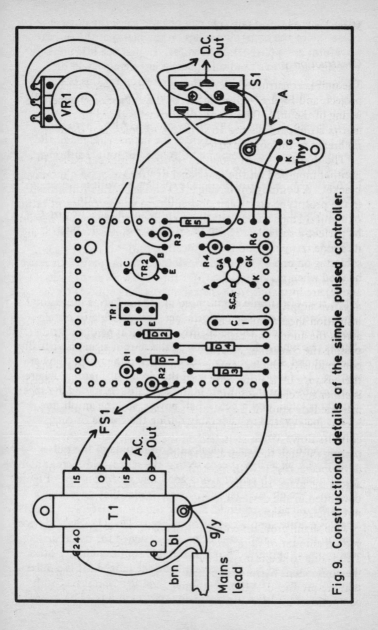

Fig. 9. Constructional details of the simple pulsed controller.

23

a limited amount of filtering can be used since the correct operation of the controller relies on the fact that the output waveform has a fairly short risetime. In practice it is unlikely that the radiation of radio frequency interference will be sufficient to merit any filtering. One reason for this is simply that the voltages involved here are quite low, so that the signals generated are nothing like as strong as those produced by controllers operating at the mains voltage. Also, there is no easy path for these signals to enter the mains wiring, and they are not likely to be propogated through this route (although they will be radiated by the railway track).

Anyway, if any problems are experienced with radio interference a small choke (of adequate current rating) can be connected in series with the output, and a capacitor of a few nano farads in value can be wired across the output sockets.

Improved Pulsed Controller

While the very simple circuit used in Figure 7 gives quite good slow speed and starting performance, it is possible to obtain even better results using a slightly different type of controller. This is one where the amplitude of the output signal is virtually constant and does not vary with changes in the output power setting. This is not the case with the circuit of Figure 7 where the amplitude of the output pulses steadily reduces as the speed control is taken down below half power, and the amplitude of the signal varies considerably during the course of each pulse.

As mentioned earlier, ideally the amplitude of the pulses should be high at low speeds so that the motor is driven at high power during each pulse, giving good low speed control. Figure 10 shows the circuit diagram of a controller that does have a constant output amplitude, and the use of an integrated circuit enables a quite simple circuit to be used. The TDA2006 device used in the IC1 position is primarily designed for use as an audio power amplifier, but it is suitable for use in many other applications, and is a very versatile device indeed. It is similar in many respects to an operational amplifier, and it has both inverting (pin 2) and non-inverting (pin 1) inputs. The main

24

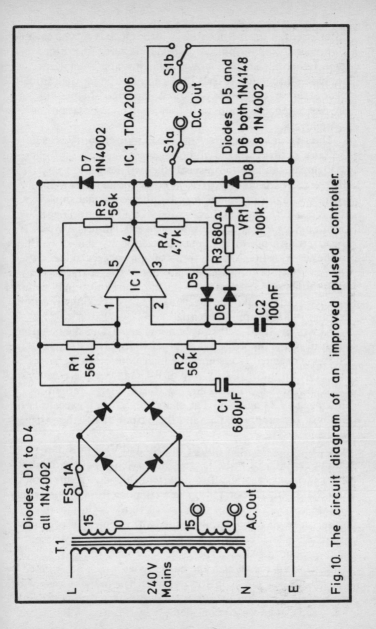

Fig.10. The circuit diagram of an improved pulsed controller.

difference is in the output stage which is a class B type capable of providing high output currents and powers. The device looks rather like a plastic power transistor at a quick glance, but closer inspection reveals that it has five rather than three leadout wires. In most applications, including the present one, the device requires no discrete frequency compensation components.

The step-down, rectifier, and smoothing circuitry is exactly the same as that featured in the Constant Voltage Controller of Figure 3, but in other respects the two designs are very different. IC1 is connected as an oscillator and uses a configuration that is often employed with operational amplifiers. R1, R2 and R5 make IC1 act rather like a Schmitt Trigger circuit having a large amount of hysteresis. In other words, if the inverting input of IC1 is taken fractionally above two thirds of the supply voltage the output at pin 4 triggers to the low state (a very low voltage), and in order to trigger the output back to the high state (virtually equal to the full supply voltage) it is necessary to take the inverting input to fractionally below one third of the supply potential.

At switch on C2 is obviously not charged, and the inverting input of IC1 is therefore at the negative supply potential. IC1's output consequently assumes the high state, and C2 charges from the output of IC1 by way of R4 and D5. The polarity of D6 is such that it prevents any significant charge current flowing via VR1 and R3. The charge on C2 soon exceeds two thirds of the supply voltage and the output of IC1 then triggers to the low state.

C2 now discharges through D6, R3 and VR1 into the output circuitry of IC1. There is no discharge path through R4 since D5 blocks any significant current flow in this direction. The charge on C2 soon falls to less than one third of the supply voltage, and IC1's output then reverts to the high state once more, causing C2 to commence charging again. This cycle of events is repeated indefinately with a rectangular waveform being produced at the output.

The time during which the output goes high is determined by the value of R4 and is obviously fixed. The period during which the output is low, on the other hand, is determined by R3 and VR1, and can be varied considerably by means of VR1.

With VR1 at maximum resistance the discharge resistance for C2 (R3 plus VR1 in series) is obviously much larger than the charge resistance (R4), giving a discharge time considerably in excess of the charge time. This means that the output is in the high state for a much shorter time than it is in the low state, giving an output waveform of the type shown in Figure 11(a). This obviously has only a low average voltage, and gives insufficient power to operate the train.

If VR1 is adjusted to the point where the resistance through VR1 and R3 is equal to the resistance of R4, the charge and discharge times of C2 become the same, as do the low and high output times. This gives an output waveform of the type shown in Figure 11(b), with a one to one mark space ratio and half power being supplied to the load.

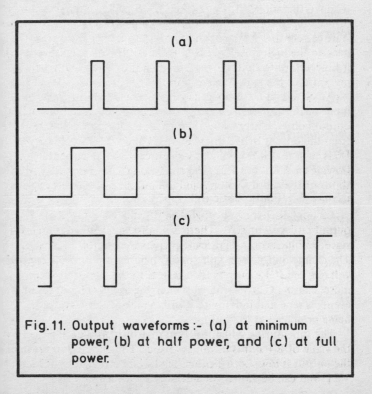

Fig. 11. Output waveforms :- (a) at minimum power, (b) at half power, and (c) at full power.

27

With VR1 at minimum resistance the space between the output pulses becomes short in relation to the length of the output pulses, and this gives an output waveform of the type shown in Figure 11(c). Here the average output level is obviously very high, and this gives full speed from the motor in the locomotive.

Note that the three waveforms of Figure 11 are not drawn using the same time scale, and that the output pulses of the controller have a fixed duration; it is only the interval between them that varies.

D7 and D8 are merely protection diodes for IC1 and do not play an active role in the operation of the circuit. S1 is the forward/reverse switch.

Components: Improved Pulsed Controller (Figure 10)

Resistors, all 1/3 watt 5%

R1	56k
R2	56k
R3	680 ohms
R4	4.7k
R5	56k

Potentiometer
VR1	100k lin carbon

Capacitors
C1	680μF 25V
C2	100nF plastic foil (type C280)

Semiconductors
IC1	TDA2006

D1 to D4 plus D7 and D8 1N4002 (6 off)
D5 to D6   1N4148 (2 off)

Switch
S1	DPDT toggle switch

Transformer
T1	Standard mains primary, twin 15 volts 1 amp secondaries

Miscellaneous
Case
0.1in matrix stripboard panel
Control knob
Output sockets
20mm 1 amp fuse and chassis mounting fuseholder to suit
Mains lead, wire, solder, etc.

Construction

This controller uses the same basic method of construction as
the previous two designs. The 0.1in matrix stripboard layout
and other wiring of the unit are illustrated in Figure 12. The
required board size is 18 copper strips by 23 holes, and there
are no breaks in the copper strips.

Since the output of IC1 does not switch between zero
volts and the full supply potential, but falls slightly short of
these two levels, it has to dissipate a significant amount of
power under certain operating conditions, and it must be
fitted with a small commercially produced, finned, bolt-on
heatsink. Alternatively it can be bolted to the case which will
act as a heatsink, and no insulating set is required as both
IC1s heat-tab and the case connect to the negative supply rail.
IC1 has built-in short circuit protection circuitry incidentally,
and this protects the unit against brief overloads and short
circuits on the output. FS1 provides protection against more
prolonged overloads. The TDA2006 also has thermal overload
protection, and should not become damaged if its heatsink
should prove to be inadequate (not that this is likely to occur
in this instance as very little heatsinking is required).

As was the case with the previous circuit, a certain amount
of radio frequency interference will be radiated by the circuit,
but this is not likely to be severe enough to warrant the
inclusion of suppression components.

Inertia/Breaking Controller

Using controllers of the type described so far is very different
from driving a real train in that inertia tends to give a real train
comparitively slow acceleration, and momentum tends to

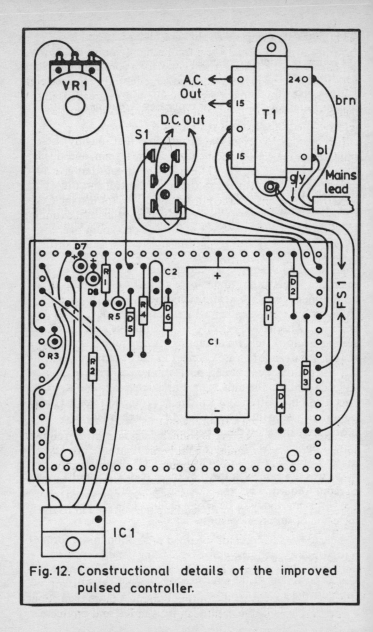

Fig. 12. Constructional details of the improved
pulsed controller.

keep the train moving once it has got under-way and is travelling at speed. Thus a real train can only move off slowly, and once it is moving fast it will coast for a considerable distance if the power is cut off. By contrast a model train can accelerate to maximum speed almost instantly due to its unrealistically high power to weight ratio, and it also tends to stop just as quickly when the power is switched off.

It is possible to design train controllers that roughly simulate the inertia and momentum of a real train, and this is achieved by including R − C filters in the circuit that give a delay between adjustments to the speed control and the appropriate response in the output signal. If, for instance, the speed control is turned as quickly as possible to maximum, the output voltage gradually builds up to maximum over a period of a few seconds, giving a relatively slow and realistic build-up in the speed of the train. If the power is then suddenly backed-off to zero, the output voltage drops back to zero over a period of perhaps 20 seconds or so. Of course, a full size train has brakes so that it does not have to simply coast to a halt, and braking can be simulated by a control that adds some resistance into the R − C circuitry to give a reduced time constant and bring the train to a stand-still more quickly.

Figure 13 shows the circuit diagram of a train controller that incorporates inertia, momentum, and braking. The circuit is basically just a constant voltage controller, with IC1 and Tr1 being connected to form a unity voltage gain buffer stage with 100% negative feedback from the emitter of Tr1 to the inverting input of IC1. Tr2 is connected as an emitter follower output stage which enables the fairly high output currents involved to be supplied by the circuit. This gives roughly unity voltage gain from the non-inverting input of IC1 to the emitter of Tr2, and the output voltage (and train speed) can therefore be controlled by controlling the voltage fed to the non-inverting input of IC1.

Tr3, R4 and R5 provide overload protection in the form of current limiting. Under normal operating conditions the voltage developed across R4 and R5 will be insufficient to switch on Tr3, and this device therefore has no significant effect on the circuit. If the output current is more than about 1 amp, this current flows through R4 and R5, and produces a

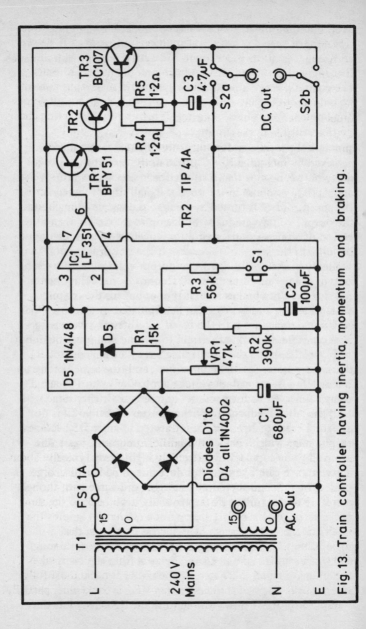

Fig. 13. Train controller having inertia, momentum and braking.

32

large enough voltage across these to bias Tr3 into conduction. This results in Tr3 pulling the non-inverting input of IC1 lower in voltage, resulting in a drop in the output voltage as well. The higher the output current becomes, the more Tr3 pulls the output voltage lower, and this results in an output current of only about 1.2 amps flowing even with a short circuit across the output. The current limiting circuit is very fast acting and gives excellent short term overload protection. Fuse FS1 protects the unit against damage due to longer overloads.

The step-down, rectifier, and smoothing circuitry is the same as that used in the previous designs, as is forward/reverse switch S2. C3 suppresses high voltage spikes developed across the motor and thus prevents them from damaging the circuit.

If R1, D5, R2, R3, C2 and S1 were to be omitted, and the slider of VR1 was connected direct to the non-inverting input of IC1, the unit would function as a straight forward constant voltage controller with VR1 being used to set the required output voltage and train speed. The additional components provide the delays so that as VR1 is operated, the output voltage does not respond immediately.

For example, if VR1 is adjusted for a steadily increasing slider voltage, this voltage is coupled to the non-inverting input of IC1 via R1 and D5. However, C2 must be charged via R1 before the voltage at IC1's input can reach the same voltage as the slider of VR1, and this gives the relatively short "inertia" delay when VR1 is used to start and accelerate the train.

When VR1 is adjusted in the opposite direction C2 is not able to discharge through D5, R1 and VR1 since D5 becomes reverse biased and blocks any significant current flow. The input impedance of IC1 is extremely high, being typically about a million megohms, and so this does not provide a discharge path either. R2 does provide a suitable discharge path though, and IC1's input voltage does eventually drop back to the same potential as VR1's slider (this circuit explanation ignores the small voltage drop through D5 which is of no practical importance). The time constant of C2 and R2 is quite long, and this gives the "momentum" delay so that the train takes a fairly long time to come to rest when VR1 is backed-off fully, and slows down only gradually when VR1 is backed-off partially.

By operating S1 it is possible to shunt R3 across R2, thus

giving a much lower discharge resistance for C2. This greatly speeds up the voltage drop across C2 (assuming VR1 has just been backed-off somewhat) and simulates applying the brakes to the train.

Thus the train is started and accelerated by advancing VR1, and is slowed down or halted by backing-off VR1 and operating S1 as necessary. This is obviously much more difficult to master than driving a model train using a controller without the inertia, momentum, and braking effects, but for most people this makes it much more challenging and much more fun.

Components: Inertia/Braking Controller (Figure 13)

Resistors, all ½ watt 5%

R1	15k
R2	390k
R3	56k
R4	1.2 ohms
R5	1.2 ohms

Potentiometer

VR1	47k lin carbon

Capacitors

C1	680μF 25V
C2	100μF 25V
C3	4.7μF 25V

Semiconductors

IC1	LF351 or TL081CP
Tr1	BFY51
Tr2	TIP41A
Tr3	BC107
D1 to D4	1N4002 (4 off)
D5	1N4148

Switches

S1	Push to make release to break type
S2	DPDT toggle switch

Transformer

T1	Standard mains primary, twin 15 volt 1 amp secondaries

Miscellaneous
Case
0.1in matrix stripboard panel
20mm 1 amp quick-blow fuse and chassis mounting fuseholder
to suit
Control knob
Output sockets, wire, solder, etc.

Construction

Once again, the controller is constructed along much the same
lines as those described earlier in this book. Most of the
components are fitted onto a 0.1in pitch stripboard which
measures 17 copper strips by 30 holes, and Figure 14 shows the
component layout of this together with details of the other
wiring. Note that this layout does, unlike the previous ones,
require a number of breaks to be made in the copper strips
prior to fitting the components in place. Figure 15 illustrates
the underside of the board and details the necessary breaks in
the strips.

Construction of the unit is quite straight forward, but be
careful not to leave out the three link wires, make sure that the
semi-conductors and electrolytic capacitors are connected with
the correct polarity, and be sure to remove any short circuits
that are produced between adjacent copper strips due to small
pieces of excess solder. Tr2 is mounted "off board", and it
must be fitted on a substantial heatsink (which can be the case
provided a metal type is used). The heat-tab of Tr2 connects
to its collector terminal, and it is necessary to use an insulating
set to ensure that it is insulated from the case. Use a continuity
tester or a multimeter set to a low ohms range to check that the
insulation is effective since a short circuit here could result in
damage to the unit.

There is plenty of room for experimentation with this circuit,
and you may, for example, prefer a faster time constant in the
inertia delay circuit. This can be achieved by reducing the value
of R1, or a slower build-up in speed can be produced by using
a higher value here. The time taken for the tain to coast to a
stand-still can be increased by increasing the value of R2, or
decreased by reducing the value of this component. Of course,

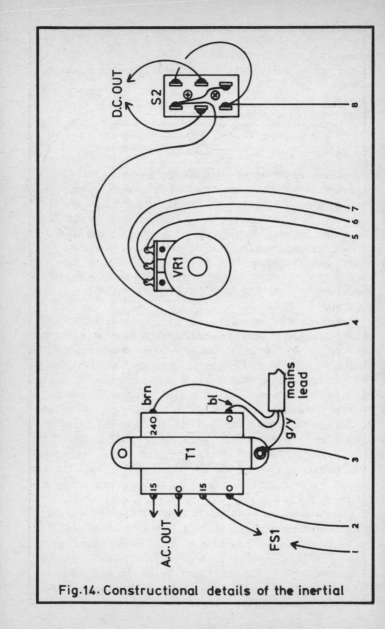

Fig.14. Constructional details of the inertial

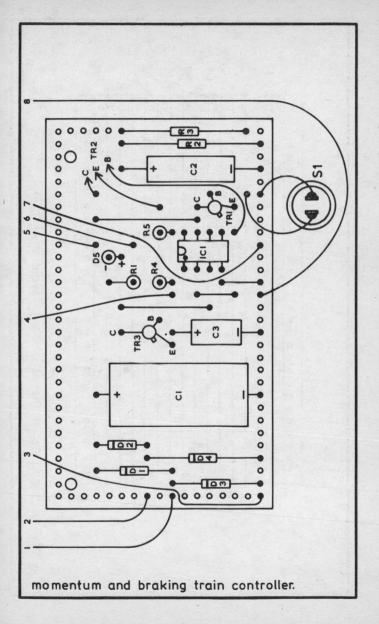

momentum and braking train controller.

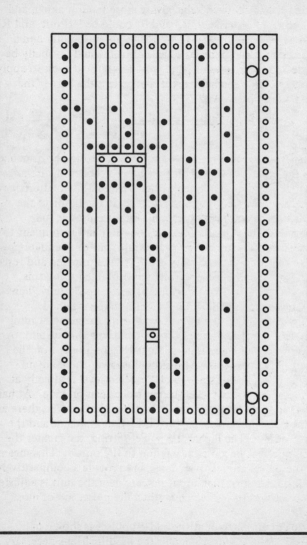

Fig. 15. The underside of the stripboard layout of Fig. 14.

R1 and (or) R3 could be replaced by variable resistors so that the time constants could be adjusted to exactly suit your requirements. The value of R3 can also be altered to change the braking speed; reduced value giving more rapid braking, and vice versa. Alternatively, R3 and S1 could be left out, and R2 could be replaced by (say) a 470k lin. potentiometer and a 39k resistor wired in series. This control would normally be adjusted to full resistance, and would be turned back to apply the brakes. The further back it is adjusted, the harder the brakes would be applied.

Pulser

It would be possible to obtain improved starting performance from the circuit of Figure 13 by adding a capacitor discharge circuit of the type described earlier (Figure 5). An alternative and more convenient method is to add an oscillator to the circuit that gives a regular train of output pulses at full amplitude. These pulses must be too brief and infrequent to give sufficient output to move the train, but of adequate power to give the train the necessary jolt to start it moving and resist stalling. The increase in performance obtained using this method is not vast (the basic circuit performs quite well anyway), but a worthwhile improvement can be attained.

Figure 16 shows the output waveforms obtained at minimum, half, and maximum power when using this system. At minimum power there is no straight DC component on the output, just the pulses. At maximum power there are no pulses on the output since the DC output level is already at the maximum output level the controller can provide. At half power, and any intermediate settings for that matter, there is a combination of a straight forward DC component and the output pulses. The higher the power setting, the greater the DC component becomes in relation to the pulses. This means that the pulses are relatively large and provide a comparitively high proportion of the output power when the unit is adjusted to low speed settings, which is when the pulses are of most benefit.

The circuit diagram of the add-on pulser is shown in Figure 17, and Figure 18 details the modifications necessary

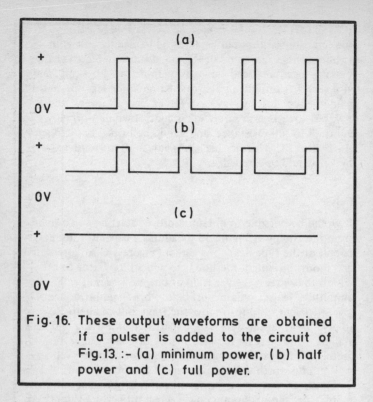

Fig. 16. These output waveforms are obtained if a pulser is added to the circuit of Fig. 13. :- (a) minimum power, (b) half power and (c) full power.

to the original controller circuit to permit the addition of the pulser.

The pulser uses the same oscillator configuration as the pulse controller circuit of Figure 10. R4 and steering diode D1 are used to give C2 a relatively short charge time and thus give a high output period which is short in comparison to the low output period. It may be found that improved results can be obtained by increasing the value of R4 somewhat to give slightly longer output pulses, but this should not be made too high or it will not be possible to halt the train!

D2 is included at the output so that when the output of the pulser goes high it is able to take the non-inverting input of IC1 in the main controller circuit (and therefore the output of the controller as well) into the high state, but when the output

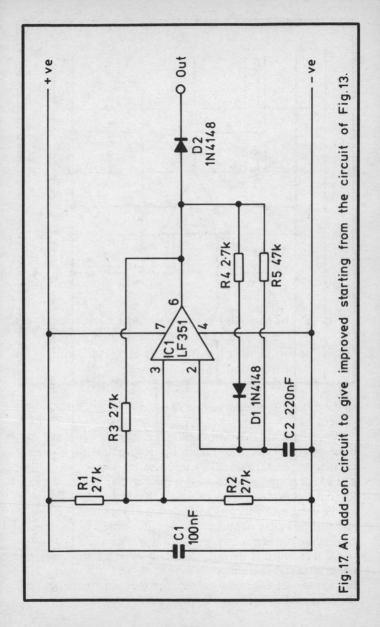

Fig.17 An add-on circuit to give improved starting from the circuit of Fig.13.

41

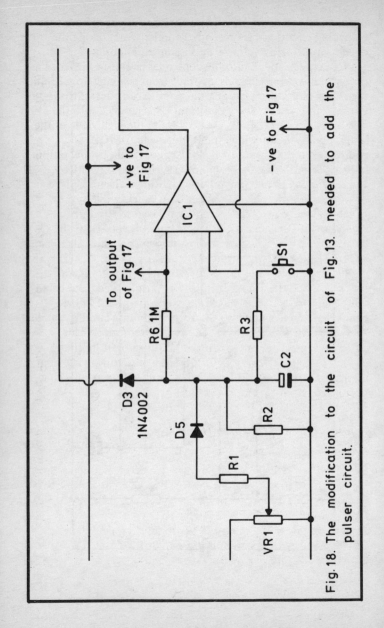

Fig. 18. The modification to the circuit of Fig. 13. needed to add the pulser circuit.

of the pulser goes low D5 effectively disconnects it from the controller circuit. This prevents the pulser from taking the output of the controller low during these periods.

R6 has been added into the controller circuit to prevent the output pulses from the pulser circuit from charging up C2 in the controller circuit, and causing the train to run constantly at virtually full speed. The signal from C2 is coupled into the non-inverting input of IC1 via R6 despite the high value of the latter, due to the very high input impedance of IC1. Of course, when the output of the pulser goes high, its low output impedance enables it to swamp the signal from C2 via R6 and take the non-inverting input of IC1 high. There will obviously be some charging effect on C2 due to the output of the pulser charging this capacitor by way of R6, but the high value of R6 and the low average output voltage of the pulser ensure that this charging is not high enough to significantly affect the performance of the controller circuitry.

When the pulser was first added to the controller it was found that the train moved straight off at top speed and could not be controlled. This was found to be due to C2 in the controller being charged via the current limiting circuitry, and so an additonal diode (D3) was added to prevent this. This diode prevents a current flowing from the current limiting circuitry into C2, but does not prevent a current flowing from C2 into the current limiting circuitry, and so the latter is able to function normally.

Components: Add-On Pulser (Figure 17)

Resistors, all 1/3 watt 5%
R1 to R3	27k (3 off)
R4	2.7k
R5	47k
R6	1M

Capacitors
C1	100nF plastic foil (type C280)
C2	220nF plastic foil (type C280)

Semiconductors
IC1	LF351

D1	1N4148
D2	1N4148
D3	1N4002

Miscellaneous
0.1in matrix stripboard
wire, solder, etc.

Construction

The pulser circuit is constructed on a 0.1in matrix stripboard having 12 copper strips by 15 holes. Both the component layout and underside of the board (including the locations of the five breaks in the copper strips) are illustrated in Figure 19. Construction of the board is quite straight forward and there should be no difficulty in fitting it into the controller as it is quite small.

It is necessary to modify the controller circuit board slightly, and the modified section of the board is shown in Figure 20. These modifications are as follows:-

A link wire is removed and R6 is connected in its place.

The collector lead of Tr3 is moved one hole further up the board.

D3 is added to the board.

The break in the copper strip to the right of the upper connection of D3 is added.

The three leads to the pulser are added.

It should perhaps be pointed out that the current limiting circuitry does not function properly during the output pulses, but in practice this does not seem to be of any real consequence, with no damage occuring if the output is briefly short circuited and a suitably low average output current being produced.

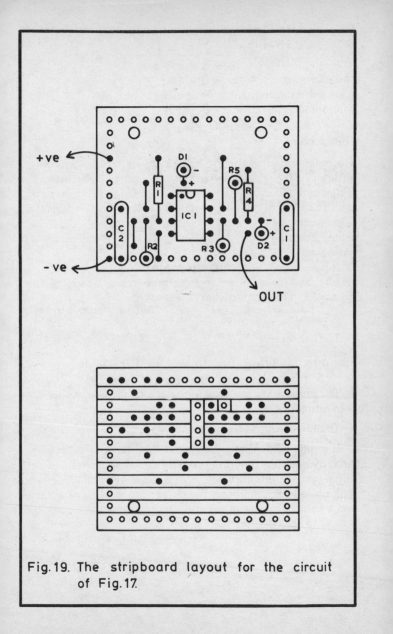

+ve

D1
−
+

R5

R1

R4

IC 1

C 2

R2

R3

D2
−
+

C 1

−ve

OUT

Fig. 19. The stripboard layout for the circuit of Fig. 17.

45

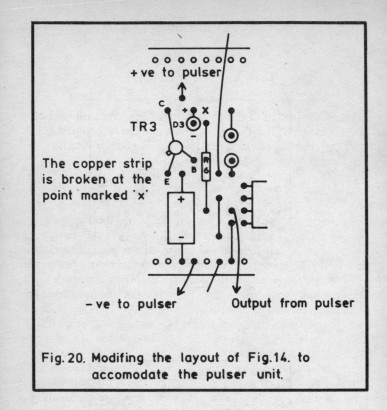

Fig. 20. Modifing the layout of Fig.14. to accomodate the pulser unit.

46

CHAPTER 2

ACCESSORIES

In this second half of the book we shall consider a number of accessories for model railways, and a number of practical projects will be described including a points controller, automatic signals, and sound effects.

Point Controller

For a large and complex layout electric points are ideal as they permit the whole system to be controlled from a single place. Even on the most simple of layouts the use of an electric point or points can make the system easier and more fun to use.

Electric points are basically quite simple devices which incorporate two solenoids (electro-magnets), one being used to set the point, and the other to reset it to its original position. In order to change the point from one setting to another it is merely necessary to apply a brief but strong burst of power to the appropriate solenoid.

A point controller can merely consist of a couple of push button switches, as shown in Figure 21. Note that although the point contains two solenoids it only has three terminals since one of these is common to both solenoids (most points have a line of three terminals, and the common one is the middle one of the three). The point will operate from an AC supply perfectly well, and so there is no need to rectify the 15 volt AC supply (derived from the auxillary output of a controller) which is used as the power source. Of course, a 12 volt DC supply is also a suitable power source.

The power is applied to the appropriate solenoid by operating PB1 or PB2. However, great care must be taken not to apply the power to a solenoid for too long as the solenoids have a low impedance and consume quite a heavy current of at least 1 amp, and quite possibly 2 amps or more. Excessive operation of one of the push button switches could easily result in the solenoid it controls being burnt out. Another problem with

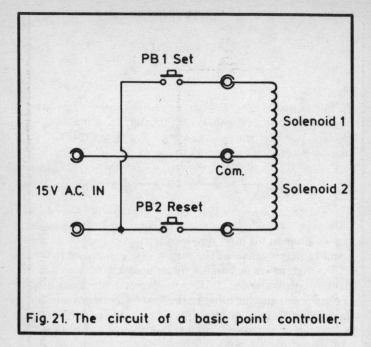

Fig. 21. The circuit of a basic point controller.

this simple arrangement is that the switches have to control quite high currents and must therefore be expensive heavy duty types if they are to achieve a useful operating life.

The Circuit

Improved results with no risk of burning out the solenoids can be obtained by using a capacitor discharge controller, and Figure 22 shows the circuit diagram of a practical controller of this type.

D1 to D4 form a bridge rectifier that produces a pulsing DC output from the AC input signal. The rough DC signal is applied to smoothing capacitor C1 by way of current limiting resistor R1. Due to the presence of R1 a maximum continuous current of only about 100mA can be supplied by the controller, and this gives a maximum output power that is inadequate to damage the solenoids in the point. Of course, this level of

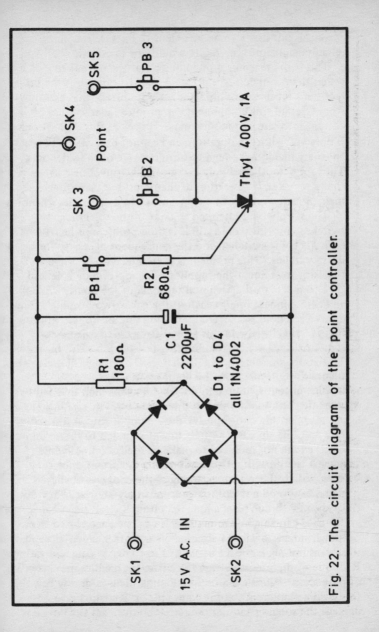

Fig. 22. The circuit diagram of the point controller.

49

current is not likely to be sufficient to operate the point reliably, and almost certainly would not operate it at all.

This is the reason for including C1 at the output side of R1, rather than connecting it direct across the output of the bridge rectifier. R1 does not limit the output current that can flow from C1, and this component can produce a large pulse of current into one of the solenoids. However, this current pulse is only very short in duration, and cannot be sustained for anything like long enough to burn out one of the solenoids. Thus the smoothed supply can give a high burst of current that gives reliable operation of the point, but cannot give a high enough continuous output power to damage the solenoids.

The supply could be used to control the solenoids via switches, but this would still leave the problem of heavy currents being switched and the consequent necessity for heavy duty switches. This problem is overcome here by the use of a thyristor to connect the supply to the appropriate solenoid. SK4 connects to the common terminal of the point, while SK3 and SK5 connect one to each of the other two terminals. The desired solenoid is selected by closing PB2 or PB3, as appropriate. PB1 is then closed and this gives a strong gate current to thyristor Thy1 via current limiting resistor R2. This biases Thy1 into conduction and discharges C1 through the selected solenoid, thus operating the point mechanism.

The current switched by PB1 is far lower than that fed to the solenoid, being something in the region of 30mA, and there is no need for this to be a heavy duty component. Admittedly PB2 and PB3 do pass the full current supplied to the solenoid, but they are not required to make or break contact while passing this current. They only pass this current once they have closed. Therefore, sparking at the contacts of these switches should not occur and even if they are not heavy duty types they should have a long operating life (all practical switches can handle a much higher current once closed than they can handle when switching on and off, incidentally).

It is not necessary to use a thyristor having a current rating of a few amps, even though the current it handles may have a peak level of as much as about 3 amps. This is simply because the current ratings normally quoted for thyristors are continuous ratings (although they may assume that the device is mounted on a large heatsink), and not peak ratings. A small (1 amp) thyristor can handle peak currents considerably in excess of its continuous rating (typically about 10 amps in fact), and such a device is therefore perfectly suitable for use here.

Once triggered to the on state a thyristor remains switched on until its anode to cathode current is reduced to a low level. This will be achieved in this case when PB2 or PB3 is released. C1 is then able to fully charge once again (assuming PB1 is also released), so that the circuit is ready to function properly again when required. This is the reason for using switches that are biased to the "off" state in the unit, and these should not be changed for non-biased types.

Although the unit is intended to be powered from an auxillary AC output of a train controller, it should also function properly if fed from a 12 volt DC auxillary output, and it can have a built-in mains transformer, if either of these alternatives are more convenient for some reason. A mains transformer having a secondary rating of 15 volts at 200mA or more is suitable to power the unit, but normal safety precautions must be observed if the unit is self-powered. The circuit **MUST NOT** be powered direct from the mains, not even via a voltage divider circuit of some kind.

Components: Point Controller (Figure 22)

Resistors
R1   180 ohms 2 watt 10%
R2   680 ohms ½ watt 5%

Capacitor
C1   2200µF 25V electrolytic

Semiconductors
Thy1   400 volt 1 amp thyristor in TO–5 can
D1 to D4   1N4002 (4 off)

Switches
PB1 to PB3 Push to make release to break type (3 off)

Miscellaneous
Case

0.1in matrix stripboard
Input and output sockets
Wire, solder, etc.

Construction

The unit is quite small and it should be possible to accommodate
it in virtually any small plastic or metal instrument case. A case
of the sloping front panel type has the advantage of convenience
in use, but it is by no means essential to employ a case of this
type.

Most of the components are mounted on a 0.1in matrix
stripboard which has 19 holes by 22 copper strips, and Figure
23 shows the component layout of this together with the small
amount of point to point fashion wiring. No breaks in the
copper strips are required using this layout. The arrangement
of the leadout wires varies from one make of thyristor to
another, and it is advisable to check the manufacturers or
retailers data before connecting this component into circuit.

Additional Outputs

As described so far the controller is only suitable for use with
a single point, but it can be readily modified for use with any
desired number of points. This merely entails adding more
output sockets and switches, as shown in Figure 24. As will
be apparent from Figure 24, three extra sockets and two push
button switches are required for each additional point. These
extra components are easily accommodated in the unit, and
no modifications to the component panel are required.

Automatic Signal

This simple circuit controls a two colour (red and green)
signal, and automatically switches this to red as the signal is
passed by a train. It is automatically reset to green again
when the train has progressed along the track to some pre-
determined point. In essence this is very similar to the
signalling systems used in full size railways, albeit in greatly
simplified form.

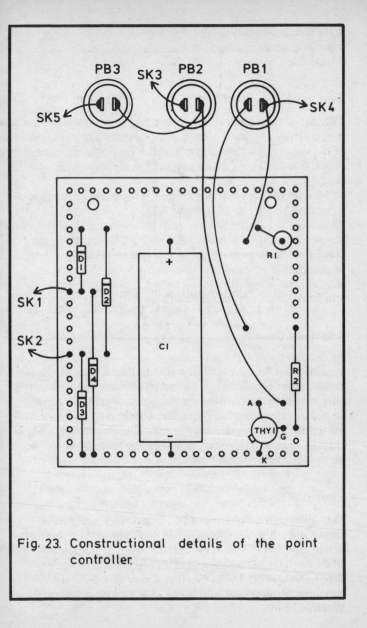

Fig. 23. Constructional details of the point controller.

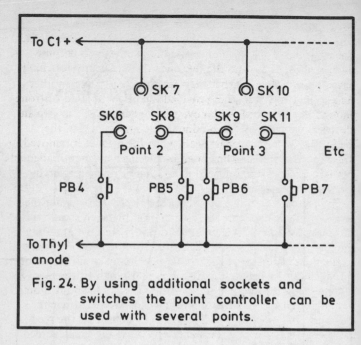

Fig. 24. By using additional sockets and switches the point controller can be used with several points.

Obviously the unit has to be able to detect that the train is passing the signal, and must also be able to detect when the train is passing the position on the layout where the signal should be reset to green. There are a great many ways of doing this, including the use of pressure switches and photo-electric switches. However, probably the least expensive and most simple method is to use a reed switch which is operated by a small permanent magnet fitted to the train.

For those who are unfamiliar with reed switches, these consist of two thin pieces of springy magnetic metal contained in a tubular glass envelope. The two pieces of metal (called "reeds") are small strips which are mounted end-to-end with a small overlap, but with a very narrow gap between the two ends. Thus under normal conditions there is no electrical connection between the two reeds due to the gap between them and the insulating mounting provided by the glass envelope. There is a leadout wire at each end of the reed switch incidentally, one connecting to each of the reeds.

A reed switch can be closed by placing a magnet close to it. The presence of the magnet causes the two reeds to become slightly magnetised, and the two ends that are nearly touching have opposite poles so that they are attracted to one another. As a springy metal is used, provided the magnetic field is strong enough, the two reeds will move together and touch to give an electrical connection. Again due to the springyness of the reeds, they will move apart again when the magnet is removed. Thus a reed switch can be closed by placing a magnet of adequate strength in close proximity to it, and can be opened again by removing the magnet.

In this system the reed switches are placed on or under the track at the places where it is desired that the train should set and reset the signal. It is possible to fit the reed switches under the track, between two sleepers, although it may be necessary to file the sleepers away slightly in order to make sufficient space for the reed switches. It is also possible to fit the reed switches lengthwise down the centre of the track, and it should be found that locomotives and rolling-stock have sufficient clearance underneath to ensure that they do not hit the reed switches. In either case it is necessary to use the smallest reed switches that can be found, and this is also advisable in the interests of obtaining reliable results since small reed switches are generally more sensitive than the larger types. An important property of reed switches in this application is that they operate a high speed, often having make and break times of less than a millisecond (a thousanth of a second) in the case of miniature types. This ensures that even when a train passes at high speed it still operates the signalling system reliably.

Although the electric motors used in model trains contain permanent magnets, these cannot be relied upon to operate the reed switches, although in a few cases it may be found that they do so and no additional magnet is required. However, in general the magnets will be too high up in the model to be effective. Bar magnets to operate reed switches are readily available and it is not difficult to fit one of these to the underside of the train. It may be possible to simply glue on the underside of the train at some point, or it may be necessary to open up either the locomotive or part of the rolling-stock so that the magnet can be fitted on the inside on the base panel. This depends upon the amount of clearance beneath the train, and how well the magnet can be concealed if it is fitted on the exterior of the train.

For maximum reliability the magnets and reed switches should be in alignment. Thus if the reed switches are fitted across the track, the magnet should be fitted across the train. If the reed switches are fitted lengthwise down the middle of the track, the magnet should be mounted lengthwise down the centre of the train.

The Circuit

The circuit of the Automatic Signal is based on a bistable multivibrator, as can be seen from the circuit diagram of Figure 25.

The unit is fed from the 15 volt auxillary output of a train controller, and D1 to D4 and C1 are used to process this to produce a DC supply for the unit.

A quite straight forward bistable circuit is used, apart from the fact that it uses VMOS transistors rather than ordinary bipolar types. VMOS devices are used as they have extremely high current gains, and are in fact voltage rather than current operated devices that comsume no significant current. The point of having this high current gain is that small filament bulbs can be used as the drain loads instead of the light emitting diodes (D5 and D6) and their series current limiting resistors (R2 and R3). Thus the unit can be entirely home-constructed using LED indicators, or can be used to control a ready-made signal incorporating small filament bulbs.

When power is initially connected to the circuit the two transistors will begin to switch on as there is a path of conduction from the positive supply to each gate. For the sake of this explanation we will assume that Tr1 starts to turn on more rapidly than Tr2, as inevitably one will have a faster risetime than the other, but there is no way of telling which will be the faster (it is of little practical importance either). As Tr1 switches on, its drain voltage is pulled lower, and this reduces the bias fed to Tr2 via R4. Thus Tr2's drain voltage tends to rise, increasing the bias to Tr1 via R1. This results in the

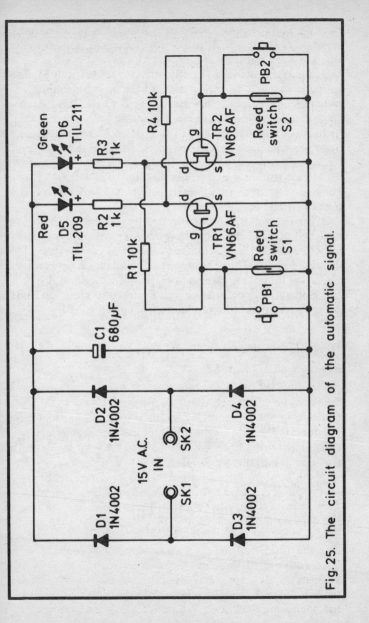

Fig. 25. The circuit diagram of the automatic signal.

57

circuit rapidly assuming the state where Tr1 is switched hard on and Tr2 is cut off. Thus D5 is switched on, D6 is switched off, and a red signal shows.

If the train passes and briefly operates reed switch S1, Tr1's gate terminal will be briefly taken to the negative supply potential and Tr1 will consequently be cut off. This causes its drain to rise to virtually the full supply potential, biasing Tr2 into conduction by way of R4. When S1 reopens again, Tr1 remains cut off as it no longer receives a gate bias from Tr2's drain which is now low. Similarly, Tr2 remains switched on since it still receives a strong bias from Tr1's drain. Thus the circuit latches with D5 switched off, D6 switched on, and a green signal being displayed.

If reed switch S2 is now operated by the train, Tr2 is switched off, and the circuit reverts to its original state, and as before, latches in that state. A red signal is therefore displayed again. Thus the required circuit action is obtained. PB1 and PB2 permit manual operation of the circuit, PB1 being operated in order to change from red to green, and PB2 being operated in order to change from green to red.

Components: Automatic Signal (Figure 25)

Resistors, all 1/3 watt 5%

R1	10k
R2	1k
R3	1k
R4	10k

Capacitor

C1	680µF 25V electrolytic

Semiconductors

D1 to D4	1N4002 (4 off)
D5	TIL209 (0.125in red LED)
D6	TIL211 (0.125in green LED)
Tr1	VN66AF
Tr2	VN66AF

Switches

PB1	push to make release to break type

PB2	push to make release to break type
S1	miniature reed switch
S2	miniature reed switch

Miscellaneous

Case

0.1in matrix stripboard panel

Two wander sockets (SK1 and SK2)

Wire, solder, etc.

Construction

Most of the components are fitted into a small metal or plastic case, but the reed switches are obviously mounted externally and are connected to the rest of the circuitry via twin leads which pass through holes drilled in the rear of the case. A further two holes are required to carry the leads to the two LEDs (D5 and D6). SK1 and SK2 are fitted to the rear panel of the case, while PB1 and PB2 are mounted on the front panel or the lid (the latter being the most convenient from the operational point of view) of the case.

The other components are assembled on a 0.1in matrix stripboard which measures 18 copper strips by 19 holes using the component layout and wiring scheme illustrated in Figure 26. There are no breaks in the copper strips. Although Tr1 and Tr2 are MOSFET devices they do not need any special handling precautions as they have internal zener protection diodes that prevent damage due to high voltage static charges.

A little ingenuity must be used when constructing the signal, and this should not be too difficult. If the circuit is used to control a ready-made signal having filament bulbs it will almost certainly be necessary to reduce R2 and R3 in value in order to obtain a high enough output current. These resistors cannot simply be replaced with shorting leads as the DC output voltage of the unit is a steady 23 volts (approximately), although this reduces somewhat if the output current of the unit is increased. However, this is still likely to be excessive and would soon burn out the bulbs in the signal. The specified values for R2 and R3 on the other hand, give a output current of only about 11mA at an output potential of 12 volts.

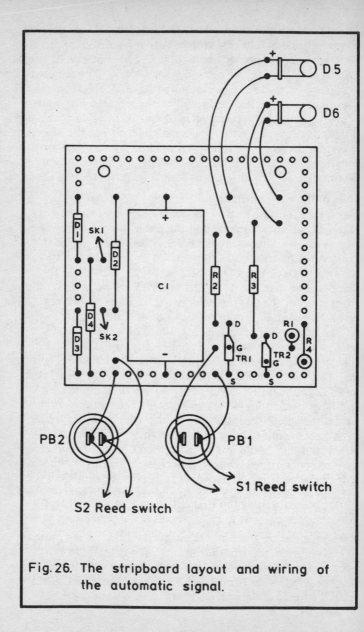

Fig. 26. The stripboard layout and wiring of
the automatic signal.

For an output voltage of 12 volts, R2 and R3 should each
have a value of 220 ohms for an output current of 50mA, 180
ohms for an output current of 60mA, 130 ohms for an output
current of 80mA, and 110 ohms for 100mA. The required value
in ohms (assuming an output potential of 12 volts is required)
is calculated by dividing 11,000 by the required current in
mA, and this gives an answer in ohms. If the calculated figure
does not coincide with a preferred value, choose the nearest
preferred value. The resistors should be 1 watt types for
currents up to 50mA, and 2 watt types for higher output
currents. The output current should be no more than about
100mA or so.

Signal Controller

This project could be regarded as the inverse of the previous
one, since it is a device that causes the train to automatically
obey a signal, rather than a signal that is controlled by the
train. Thus, if you set the signal to red the train will come to
rest just in front of the signal. Setting the signal to green
causes the train to pull away and continue its journey again. If
the signal is at green when the train is approaching, the train
moves straight past and is unaffected. Neither the drawing to a
halt or accelerating away from the signal are too abrupt, and
this is achieved by using the unit in conjunction with a train
controller having simulated inertia, momentum, and braking.
In fact this project is an add-on circuit for the train controller
circuit of Figure 13, which was described earlier.
    At first thought one might think that all this project has to
do is to stop the train when the signal is at red, and start it
again when it is at green, but is is not quite as simple as this.
The train only needs to stop when the signal is at red, and the
train is approaching the signal. The train should not stop
wherever it happens to be just because the signal is set to red!
This makes it necessary to incorporate into the circuit
something that warns the unit if the train is approaching the
signal. This is achieved using a reed switch on or under the
track, plus a permanent magnet fitted to the train, as was the
case with the previous project.

The Circuit

Figure 27 shows the full circuit diagram of the unit. Like the previous project, this one is based on a bistable multivibrator. In this case a standard bipolar transistor circuit is used, and this is comprised of Tr3, Tr4 and R5 to R8. Bistable operation was covered in the previous section of this book and will not be repeated in detail again here.

With S1 in the "green" position S1a short circuits the base of Tr4 to the negative supply rail so that Tr4 is switched off and Tr3 is biased into saturation by R5 and R7. This results in a very low potential at Tr3's collector,so that both Tr1 and Tr2 are cut off. These therefore have no effect on the controller circuitry to which they are connected, and the controller functions normally.

With S1 in the "red" position the short circuit is removed from the base of Tr4, but this does not have any affect on the state of the bistable until the train operates reed switch S2 and shorts the base of Tr3 to the negative supply, thus triggering the bistable to the other state. Of course, operations of S2 are ineffective with S1 in the "green" position since S1a disconnects S2, and the momentary operation of S2 as the train passes would be of little consequence anyway.

With the bistable triggered to the state where Tr3 is switched off and Tr4 is switched on, Tr2 is biased hard into conduction by R6 and R4, while Tr1 is biased into conduction by R6 and R2. R1 is a resistor which is connected in series with VR1 of the train controller circuit, and under normal conditions the only affect this has is to slightly (and insignificantl' reduce the maximum output voltage of the controller. However, with Tr1 switched on, the voltage at the junction of R1 and VR1 is pulled down to just a fraction of a volt, and the throttle control of the train is effectively at minimum power, regardless of the setting of VR1.

Due to the simulated momentum of the train this does not bring the train to a very rapid halt, and this makes it difficult to bring the train to rest at roughly the right spot. It would be an excessively long drawn out stop anyway, and it is necessary to operate the simulated braking circuitry in order to obtain more realistic and predictable results.

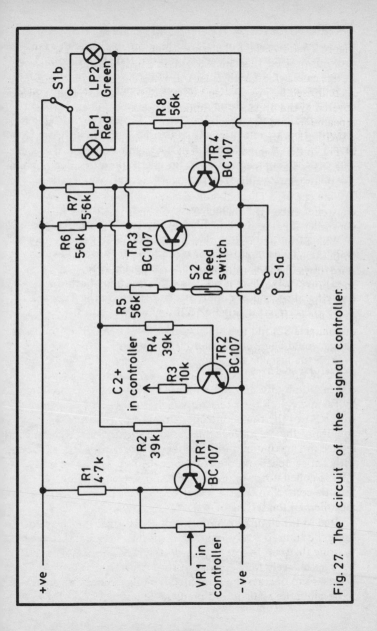

Fig. 27. The circuit of the signal controller.

63

This is achieved by Tr2 and R3 which are shunted across C2 in the controller circuit, and therefore discharge this fairly rapidly to give a reasonable fast but not too abrupt stop. The time taken for the train to stop is controlled by the value of R3, increased value giving increased stopping time, and reduced value giving a more abrupt stop.

When S1 is returned to the "green" position the bistable is triggered back to its original state as the short circuit from Tr4's base to the negative supply rail is reintroduced. Tr1 and Tr2 are then switched off, and the charge on C2 gradually builds up once again, resulting in the train smoothly accelerating away.

S1b controls the signal lamps which can either be LEDs with 1k series resistors, or filament bulbs with dropper resistors of the appropriate value. The method of finding the correct value for the dropper resistor is the same as for the previous project in this book and will not be repeated here.

Incidentally, there is no reason for not using both this circuit and the pulser circuit of Figure 17 with the Train Controller circuit of Figure 13 if you wish to do so.

Components: Signal Controller (Figure 27)

Resistors, all 1/3 watt 5%

R1	4.7k
R2	39k
R3	10k
R4	39k
R5	56k
R6	5.6k
R7	5.6k
R8	56k

Semiconductors
Tr1 to Tr4 BC107 (4 off)

Switches

S1	DPDT toggle type
S2	Miniature reed switch

Miscellaneous
0.1in matrix stripboard

Wire, solder, etc.

Construction

The additional circuitry is housed in the controller unit, and it is necessary to add a mounting hole for S1 and fit this component in place. It is also necessary to drill an exit hole for the leads to reed switch S2 and the two signal lamps. R1 is added in the positive supply lead to VR1 of the controller, and is simply mounted on the appropriate tag of VR1. The other components are mounted on a 0.1in pitch stripboard which measures 18 copper strips by 11 holes. Figure 28 shows the layout of this board together with all the other wiring (and the modified wiring to VR1 of the controller). There should be no problem in finding a suitable spot for the finished component panel inside the controller as the board is quite small.

The positive supply for the signal circuit is taken from the controller board, and the hole to the right of the one connecting to C1's positive terminal is a suitable take-off point. Similarly, the negative supply for the signal can be taken from the hole on the controller board that is just to the right of the one which connects to C1's negative leadout wire. One output of the signal board connects to VR1, as shown in Figure 28, and the other connects to the controller board at the hole between those which connect to C2's positive lead and the upper leadout of R2.

The reed switch should be positioned at a point on the track that causes the train to stop just in front of the signal when the latter is set to red and the speed control is set to maximum. This position can simply be found by trial and error, and does not take long. When the train is moving slowly and it is stopped by switching the signal to red it is likely that the train will stop some distance short of the signal, and there is no easy way of overcoming this. However, it is of no real consequence anyway since real trains do not stop at some precise distance in front of signals.

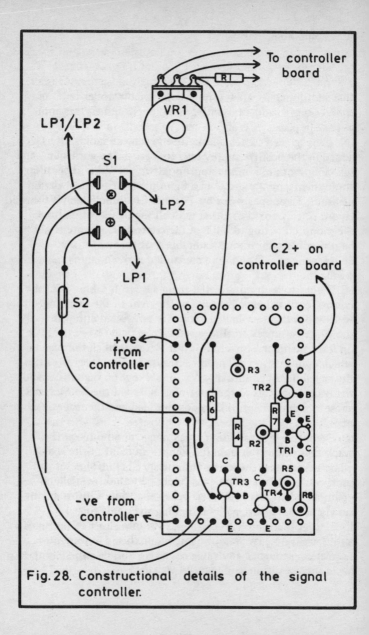

Fig. 28. Constructional details of the signal controller.

Electronic Steam Whistle

When used in conjunction with a suitable amplifier and speaker this circuit gives a simulation of a steam train whistle. Although you might think that a simple tone generator is all that is required in order to give a reasonably accurate simulation of a steam whistle, things are not really as simple as that.

One problem with a simple tone generator is that it has almost instant attack and decay, whereas a steam whistle builds up to full volume relatively slowly, remains at that level for a time, and then dies away to nothing over a short period of time. There are no precise rise and fall times which we should try to simulate since the characteristics of some whistles are very different to the characteristics of others, and there is a considerable degree of latitude available here.

Another characteristic of steam whistles is a change in tone during the rise and fall times, with the tone usually rising in pitch during the rise-time, and falling in pitch during the fall-time. However, some produce a fall in tone as the volume builds-up, and a rise in tone as it dies away, and either is acceptable in a unit of this type.

A third characteristic of a steam whistle which must be taken into account is that the purity of the note changes during the rise and fall times. Initially the note is very pure and is virtually a sinewave, but as it builds-up in volume an increase in the harmonics (multiples of the fundamental frequency) occurs. As the signal decays the opposite occurs with the harmonic levels diminishing much more rapidly than the amplitude of the fundamental signal.

One final characteristic of importance is that there is a background "hissing" sound produced by the steam which operates the whistle, and it is necessary to mix a noise of this type into the tone signal in a simulator of this type.

Obviously a circuit to produce a very precise simulation of a steam whistle could and probably would be an extremely complex one, but it is possible to obtain quite a good simulation using a relatively simple circuit such as the one described here.

The Circuit

The full circuit diagram of the Steam Whistle simulator is shown in Figure 29, and the circuit really breaks down into three sections: the tone generator, the noise generator, and a mixer which combines the two signals.

Tr1 is used as the basis of the tone generator, and this is used in a simple phase shift oscillator. Tr1 is used as a high gain common emitter amplifier having R2 and R3 to provide base biasing and act as the collector load respectively. R1, VR1 the input impedance of Tr1, and C2 to C4 act as a phase shift network which gives a phase inversion at a particular frequency. There is a phase inversion through Tr1, and so the two phase inversions cancel one another out to give positive feedback at the operating frequency of the phase shift network. The gain of Tr1 more than compensates for the losses through the phase shift network, and there is sufficient feedback to produce oscillation.

With VR1 at or around maximum resistance there is sufficient feedback to cause the circuit to oscillate strongly, producing fairly strong harmonics on the output (although the output waveform is a slightly distorted sinewave, and is far from being square). Adjusting VR1 for decreased resistance increases the losses through the phase shift network, giving an increase in the purity of the output tone. It also results in the output rising in pitch as VR1 is adjusted. If VR1 is taken too low in resistance the losses through the network become too great to permit oscillation and the signal decays.

In practice VR1 is adjusted to a setting that is just high enough in value to give reasonably strong oscillation and a noticeable harmonic content on the output. When PB1 is operated, power is applied to the circuit via the R − C circuit comprised of R4 and C1. This gives a gradual build-up in the supply voltage to the oscillator taking about half a second or so for the full supply voltage to be achieved. This tends to limit the maximum output from the tone generator when PB1 is first depressed, and gives the required build-up in volume. As the supply potential is initially building-up, Tr1 is operating at a lower collector current than normal and therefore has reduced gain. This results in the circuit oscillating less strongly initially,

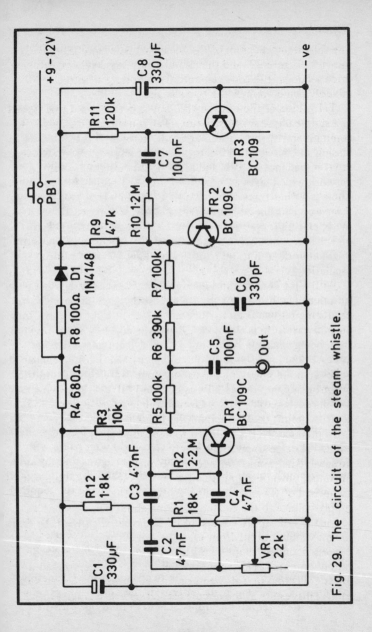

Fig. 29. The circuit of the steam whistle.

69

with the output consequently having higher purity. Thus, in addition to the gradual rise in volume, the gradual reduction in output purity and increase in harmonic content is obtained.

When PB1 is released the voltage across C1 decays, causing the output amplitude of the oscillator to gradually fall away and the purity of the tone to improve. R12 ensures that the decay time is reasonably short, and this component is essential as a decay time of several seconds is obtained if it is omitted!

The noise signal is generated by R11 and Tr3, with the reverse bias base-emitter junction of Tr3 acting rather like a zener diode. Like a zener diode it produces noise spikes, but the amount of noise seems to be higher than is obtained using a zener. Although one normally expects low currents and low noise audio transistors to produce low audio noise levels, in this circuit configuration it seems to be low currents and low noise audio devices that furnish the highest noise output levels. A BC109 device was used in the Tr3 position on the prototype, but any high gain silicon npn transistor should give good results, and most constructors will probably be able to find a suitable device in the spares box.

The output from the noise generator is not very great, being just a few millivolts RMS, and Tr2 is therefore used as a high gain common emitter amplifier which boosts the noise signal to a more acceptable level. The noise generator is fed from the main supply via R8, D1 and C8; these components giving a very rapid attack to the noise signal, as is the case with a real steam whistle. D1 prevents C8 from discharging through R8, R4 etc. when PB1 is released so that a longer decay time for the noise signal is produced, and this R – C circuit does interfere with the one in the tone generator circuitry. This gives a decay time which is much longer than the attack time, and the noise should sustain for at least as long as the tone signal, giving the required effect.

The output from the noise generator contain an excessive high frequency content and R7 plus C6 are therefore used as a simple R – C topcut filter which reduces the high frequency content to the appropriate level. R5 and R6 form a simple passive mixer which combines the two signals, and C5 merely provides DC blocking at the output of the unit.

The circuit requires a supply potential of about 9 to 12 volts, and the supply should not be much less than about 9 volts since it might then fail to reach the reverse base-emitter breakdown voltage of Tr3, and the noise signal would not be generated. The supply current is only about 1.5mA, and a small 9 volt battery (PP3 size) is probably the most practical power source.

Ideally the circuit should feed into an amplifier having a fairly high input impedance and low sensitivity, and an input intended for use with a crystal or ceramic pick-up is very suitable. The circuit also seems to work quite well with amplifiers having a lower input impedance but higher sensitivity, and it should be possible to use the unit success-fully with virtually any amplifier.

To some extent the characteristics of the signal produced by the unit are adjustable by altering the values of various components. The attack and decay times of the tone generator can be increased or decreased by altering the value of C1, with increased value giving longer attack and decay times, and reduced value giving shorter times. The decay time can be lengthened without significantly affecting the attack time by increasing the value of R12. It can also be shortened by reducing the value of R12, but this should not be reduced in value very much as the potential divider action across R4 and R12 might then reduce the supply voltage to the tone generator to an insufficient level. The amount of noise signal added into the tone generator's output can be varied by means of R6, with increased value giving reduced noise injection, and decreased value giving greater noise injection. The tone generator operates at a frequency of about 1kHz, but this can be changed by altering the values of C2 to C4. The operating frequency is inversely proportional to the values of these components.

Components: Steam Whistle (Figure 29)

Resistors, all 1/3 watt 5% (10% over 1M)

R1	18k
R2	2.2M
R3	10k
R4	680 ohms
R5	100k

R6	390k
R7	100k
R8	100 ohms
R9	4.7k
R10	1.2M
R11	120k
R12	1.8k

Potentiometer

VR1	22k lin carbon

Capacitors

C1	330µF 16V electrolytic
C2, C3 C4	4.7nF ceramic plate (3 off)
C5	100nF polyester (type C280)
C6	330pF ceramic plate
C7	100nF polyester (type C280)
C8	330µF 16V electrolytic

Semiconductors

Tr1	BC109C
Tr2	BC109C
Tr3	BC109 (see text)
D1	1N4148

Switch

PB1	Push to make, release to break type

Miscellaneous

Case
0.1in matrix stripboard
output socket (3.5mm jack, etc)
Control knob
Wire, solder, etc.

Construction

Virtually any small metal or plastic case should be adequate to house the unit and the PP3 size battery. VR1, PB1 and the output socket are mounted on the front panel or lid of the unit, and a 3.5mm jack was used as the output socket on the prototype. However, any preferred type of audio connector can of course be employed here.

The other components are wired onto a stripboard which has 15 copper strips by 30 holes and 0.1in pitch. This is illustrated in Figure 30 which also shows the small amount of point to point style wiring. Note that there are four breaks in the copper strips to be made before the components are mounted and soldered into place.

The optimum setting for VR1 can only be found by trial and error. Too low a value will cause the tone generator to barely achieve oscillation, giving a low output level and a signal lacking the right characteristics. Too high a resistance setting will give excessively strong oscillation so that the required change in tone purity during the rise and fall times does not occur. There should be a small range of intermediate settings which give the desired effect.

Two Tone Horn

This extremely simple device gives a rough simulation of the two tone horns fitted to diesel locomotives. These usually produce an initial tone of low purity and rapid rise-time, followed by a tone of similar purity and about 50% higher in pitch. The second tone is usually of relatively short duration and has a fall time which is somewhat longer than the rise-time of the signal.

The Circuit

The complete circuit diagram of the unit is shown in Figure 31, and as can be seen from this, the unit is based on the well known 555 timer IC used in the standard astable (free running oscillator) configuration. This circuit has a sufficiently powerful output to drive a high impedance loudspeaker at good volume, and it is not necessary to use a separate amplifier (although the output can be coupled to an amplifier and loudspeaker if increased volume is required).

IC1 oscillates by first charging C1 to two thirds of the supply voltage via R2 and R3, and then discharging C1 to one third of the supply voltage through R3 and an internal transistor of IC1. The output of the device is at pin 3, and this goes high while C1 is charging, and low when it is discharging. A rectangular wave-

73

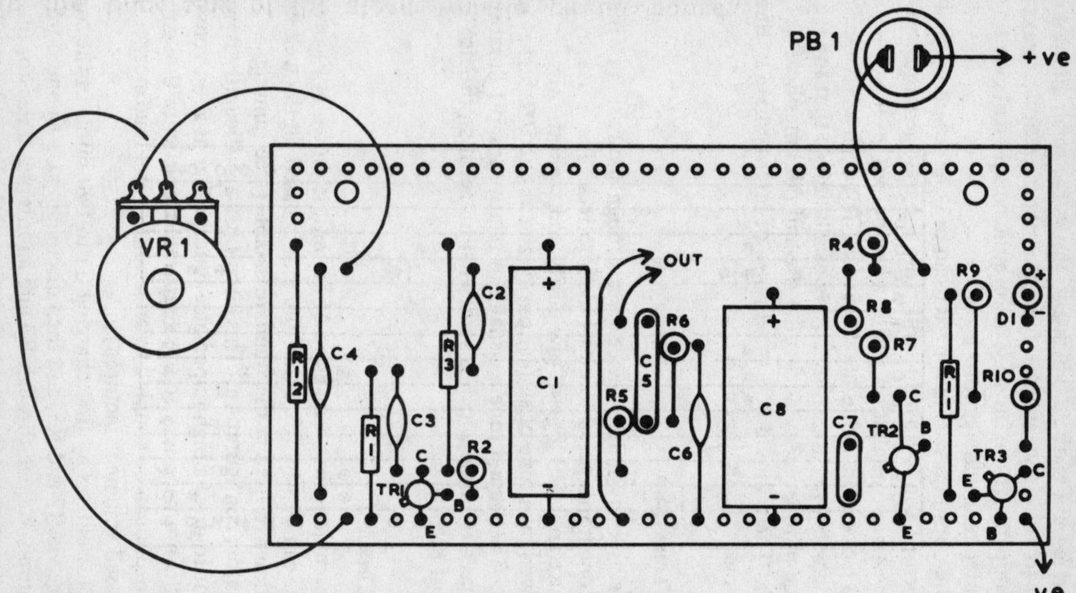

Fig. 30a. Constructional details of the steam whistle.

74

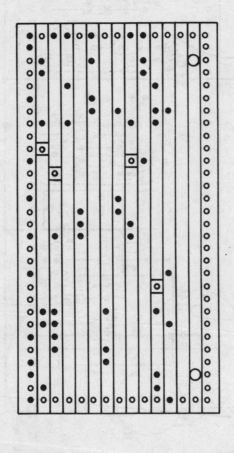

Fig. 30b. Underside of the steam whistle circuit board.

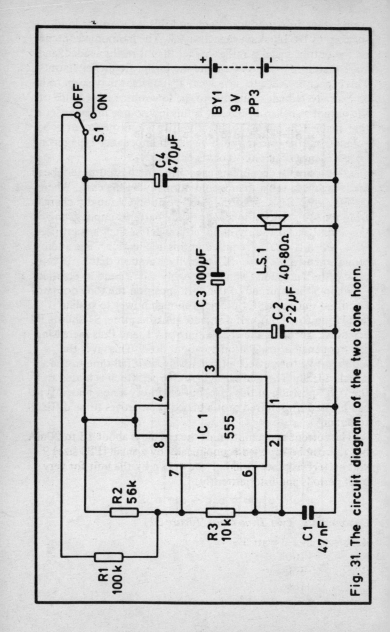

Fig. 31. The circuit diagram of the two tone horn.

form is therefore produced here, and this is fed to the loud-speaker via DC blocking capacitor C3. The harmonic content on the output signal is rather higher than is really needed, and C2 is therefore used to attenuate the higher frequency harmonics. This capacitor needs to have what at first sight may seem to be an excessively high value, due to the low source impedance of the output signal from IC1. It is this low source impedance that enables the circuit to directly drive a loudspeaker at good volume, but the speaker must be a high impedance type having an impedance of about 40 ohms or more.

C4 is a supply decoupling capacitor, and has purposely been made higher in value than would normally be the case. When on/off switch S1 is set to the "on" position C4 rapidly charges from the low source impedance of the battery supply giving the output signal a fairly rapid, although less than instant rise-time, which is what is required in this application. The audio tone is then emitted from LS1 for the duration that S1 is kept on the "on" position (which is roughly one second in practice).

When S1 is returned to the "off" position the tone does not cut off at once since C4 provides enough power to sustain oscillation for about half a second. Furthermore, S1 shunts R1 across R2, reducing the charge time of C1, and thus increasing the frequency of oscillation by about 50%. This gives the required two tone effect and relatively slow fall-time to the signal. Ideally S1 should be a biased type, which is biased to the "off" position in this case, but obviously a non-biased type can be used if preferred or if a biased type proves to be difficult to obtain.

The current consumption of the circuit is about 18 to 20mA, but this can be supplied economically by a small (PP3 size) 9 volt battery as power will only be drawn by the unit for very brief periods and intermittently.

Components: Two Tone Horn (Figure 31)

Resistors, all 1/3 watt 5%

R1	100k
R2	56k
R3	10k

Capacitors

C1	47nF polyester (type C280)
C2	2.2μF 25V electrolytic
C3	100μF 10V electrolytic
C4	470μF 10V electrolytic

Semiconductors

IC1	555

Switch

S1	SPDT toggle, preferably biased one way

Loudspeaker

LS1	Miniature type having an impedance in the range 40 to 80 ohms

Miscellaneous

0.1in matrix stripboard
Case
PP3 size battery and connector to suit
Wire, solder, etc.

Construction

The unit is housed in a small metal or plastic case with S1 and
the loudspeaker mounted on the front panel. The loudspeaker
requires a grille, and this is probably produced most easily by
drilling a matrix of small holes. Miniature speakers rarely have
any provision for fixing screws, and this leaves little option to
gluing it in place using a good quality general purpose adhesive
(quick-set epoxy types are ideal). Be careful not to use
excessive adhesive though, as the operation of the speaker
could be impaired if adhesive finds its way onto the diaphragm.

Apart from the battery the other components are wired
onto a 0.1in pitch stripboard which measures 12 copper strips
by 21 holes. Details of this board and the other wiring of the
unit are illustrated in Figure 32. This is all very simple and
straight forward, but be careful not to overlook the four
breaks in the copper strips which should be made prior to
connecting IC1, and the five link wires.

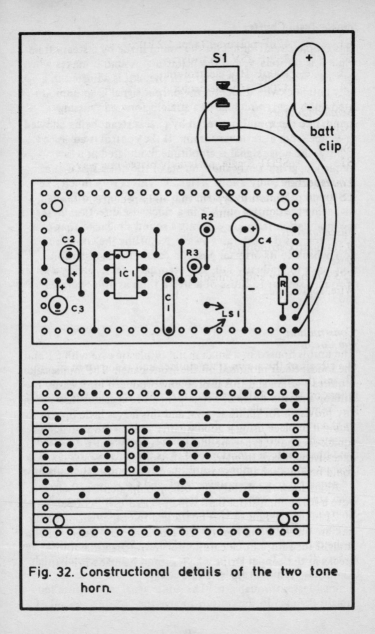

Fig. 32. Constructional details of the two tone horn.

Simple Train Chuffer

This simple circuit simulates the sound made by a steam train while it is stationary, and the "chuffing" sound it makes when moving. When the main control of the unit is adjusted in a fully anticlockwise direction the output signal is an unmodulated noise signal which gives a straight forward "hissing" sound, like the sound produced by excess steam being allowed to escape from a stationary train. If the control is advanced slightly, the noise signal is amplitude modulated at a low frequency, giving fairly short bursts of the noise signal at a low frequency (only about 1 Hertz). This is very much like the sound produced by a train as it starts to move off, and advancing the control further in a clockwise direction increases the modulation frequency, giving a sound similar to that of a steam train as it accelerates away. Adjusting the control slowly back to its original position causes the modulation frequency to gradually fall, and eventually cease, giving a series of sounds similar to those of a steam train as it decelerates and stops.

The Circuit

The circuit of the steam train chuffer unit is shown in Figure 33, and this breaks down into three main sections; a noise generator, an amplitude modulator, and a variable frequency, low frequency oscillator.

The noise generator is similar to the one employed in the steam whistle project described earlier, and uses the reversed biased base-emitter junction of Tr4 as the noise source. Tr3 is used as a common emitter amplifier which boosts the output of the generator to an acceptable level, and C4 is used to give a small amount of treble cut to this stage as the noise signal otherwise has an excessive high frequency content.

The modulator is based on Tr2, and the noise signal is fed to the collector of Tr2 by way of DC blocking capacitor C3 and resistor R6. If Tr2 is switched off, there is an extremely high impedance from its emitter to its collector, and there are minimal losses through R6. The noise signal is therefore fed straight through to the output to give the "hissing" sound of a

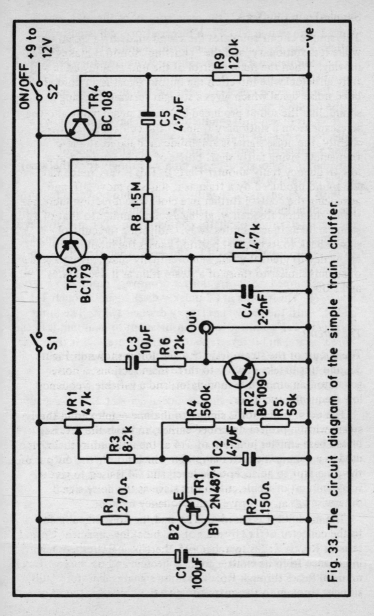

Fig. 33. The circuit diagram of the simple train chuffer.

stationary train. VR1 is the main control of the unit, and is ganged with switch S1. When this control is adjusted fully anticlockwise S1 is in the open position and cuts off the power to the modulation oscillator. This prevents any forward bias from being fed to Tr2's base, ensuring that it remains cut off and that the noise signal is indeed fed through to the output in the required manner.

If Tr2 is biased into conduction it will have quite a low collector to emitter impedance, resulting in the noise signal being attenuated to some degree. The precise degree of attenuation obviously depends on how strongly (or otherwise) Tr2 is forward biased.

With VR1 advanced slightly, S1 closes and power is fed to the modulation oscillator. This uses a unijunction transistor in the usual relaxation oscillator configuration. Tr1 initially has a very high input impedance to its emitter terminal, allowing C2 to charge up via VR1 and R3. However, when the charge on C2 reaches about 80% of the supply potential Tr1 "fires" and the input impedance at its emitter drops very rapidly to a very low level. This results in C2 quickly discharging through Tr1 and R2 until the charge has largely drained away. The input voltage to Tr1's emitter is then insufficient to maintain it in the "fired" state, and it reverts to its original state. C2 is then able to charge up once again via VR1 and R3 until the charge voltage is sufficient to trigger Tr1 once again.

This cycle of events repeats itself indefinately with a sort of sawtooth waveform being produced across C2. The signal builds up steadily as C2 charges, and drops back again sharply as it discharges. This signal is coupled to the base of Tr2 where it causes a sudden burst of noise from the output as the charge voltage quickly drops and Tr2 switches off, followed by a more gradual fall off in the output signal level as the charge on C2 increases and Tr2 switches on. This gives quite a realistic chuffing effect.

Initially VR1 will have quite a high value, giving a fairly long charge time for C2 and a consequent low frequency of oscillation (and chuffing rate). Advancing VR1 results in a reduction of its resistance and the speeding up of the chuffing rate, with a frequency of several Hertz being achieved at full advancement and minimum resistance.

S2 is the ordinary on/off switch and is the only other control in the circuit. The circuit has a current consumption of only about 2mA and requires a supply voltage of about 9 to 12 volts. The unit can be powered from a small 9 volt battery (PP3 size), but Tr4 must be a device having a fairly low reverse emitter — base breakdown voltage or the unit may fail to work when the battery voltage drops slightly due to ageing. Tr4 does not have to be the specified type, and any high gain silicon npn device should work in the circuit. Most constructors will probably be able to find a suitable device in their spares box.

Like the steam whistle project described earlier, the output of the unit should preferably be fed to an insensitive input having a high input impedance (the ceramic cartridge input of an amplifier is again ideal), but it can be used with amplifiers having higher sensitivity and a comparitively low input impedance. For best results with an amplifier of the latter type though, it will probably be necessary to add a resistor of about 100k in series with the output of the chuffer unit.

Components: Simple Train Chuffer (Figure 33)

Resistors, all 1/3 watt 5% (10% over 1M)

R1	270 ohms
R2	150 ohms
R3	8.2k
R4	560k
R5	56k
R6	12k
R7	4.7k
R8	1.5M
R9	120k

Potentiometer

VR1	47k lin carbon with switch (S1)

Capacitors

C1	100µF 16V electrolytic
C2	4.7µF 25V electrolytic
C3	10µF 25V electrolytic
C4	2.2nF polystyrene
C5	4.7µF 25V electrolytic

Semiconductors

Tr1	2N4871
Tr2	BC109C
Tr3	BC179
Tr4	BC108

Switches

S1	Part of VR1
S2	SPST miniature toggle type

Miscellaneous

Case
Control knob
0.1in matrix stripboard
Output socket (3.5mm jack or similar)
Wire, solder, etc.

Construction

Once again, only a small metal or plastic box is needed to house the project. VR1, S2 and the output socket are fitted on the lid or front panel, and the rest of the components are fitted onto a 0.1in matrix stripboard which has 16 copper strips by 20 holes. The component layout and point to point wiring are shown in Figure 34, while the underside of the board is illustrated in Figure 35. Note that there is just a single break in one of the copper strips.

The characteristics of the sound produced by the unit can be varied to some extent to suit individual tastes and requirements. For example, a lower pitched sound can be obtained by increasing C4 in value, or a higher pitched signal can be achieved by reducing or removing C4. If the "chuffing" sounds seem quiet compared to the stationary "hissing" sound it might be found beneficial to make R5 slightly lower in value. Alternatively, if the modulation seems to be lacking in depth, raising the value of R5 slightly should be of benefit.

Automatic Chuffer

Although the chuffer circuit of Figure 33 gives quite effective results, it has the obvious drawback that it is necessary to

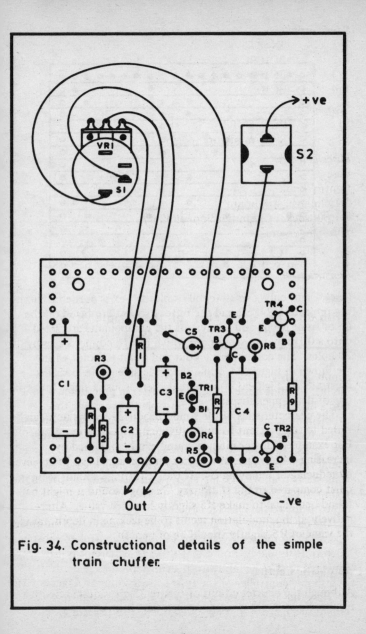

Fig. 34. Constructional details of the simple train chuffer.

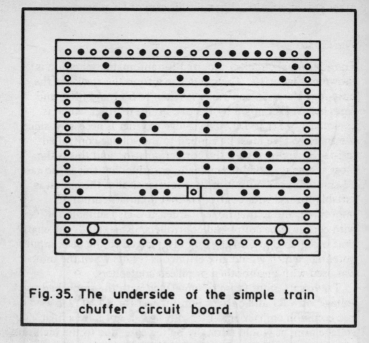

Fig. 35. The underside of the simple train chuffer circuit board.

simultaneously operate the train controller and the chuffer circuit, which is quite difficult to master in practise, and is also a little inconvenient. It is possible to overcome this problem by using a slightly more sophisticated chuffer circuit which has the chuffing rate controlled by the voltage across the tracks. If correctly set up, this results in a steady "hissing" sound while the train is stationary, a low chuffing rate as the train starts to move off, increasing to a fast chuffing rate as the train reaches full speed, without the need for any manual adjustments to the chuffer circuit.

The chuffer unit of Figure 33 is easily modified to automatic operation by replacing VR1 with a voltage controlled resistance circuit. It should be noted that this add-on circuit is primarily intended to take its input from a constant voltage controller, or a simple controller of the type shown earlier in Figures 1 and 2. However, it also works well with the pulsed controller circuit of Figure 7, and may well operate satisfactorily with

86

other pulsed circuits, although this cannot be guaranteed.

The Circuit

The additional circuitry required for automatic operation is
shown in Figure 36. The input signal from the tracks or the
output of the train controller is taken to SK1 and SK2, and
from here it is coupled by R5 to a bridge rectifier which is
comprised of D1 to D4. The bridge rectifier is necessary since
the track voltage must be applied to the voltage controlled
resistance circuitry with the correct polarity, and this is the
most simple way of automatically ensuring that this is the case.
C1 smoothes the output of the rectifier so that the circuit is
suitable for use with controllers that do not incorporate
smoothing, and as mentioned earlier, it is also suitable for use
with certain types of pulsed controllers. R5 extends the charge
time of C1 so that C1 is not simply charged to the peak input
potential, which would give erroneous results when the unit
was used with unsmoothed or pulsed controllers.

Tr2 has its input (base terminal) fed with the smoothed track
voltage via VR1 and current limiting resistor R4. Tr2 is used
as a common emitter amplifier, but it does not have a high
voltage gain, as would normally be the case, due to the inclusion
of unbypassed emitter resistor R3 and the large amount of
negative feedback it introduces. In fact Tr2 has a voltage gain
of only about unity, and being a common emitter stage it gives
a phase inversion. Thus, with the track voltage low Tr2 is cut
off and it has a collector voltage virtually equal to the supply
voltage. As the track voltage (and Tr2's base voltage) are
raised, Tr2 conducts more heavily and its collector potential
gradually decreases until it falls to virtually the negative supply
potential.

Tr1 has its collector to emitter impedance connected in
place of VR1 in the original chuffer circuit, and it is used as a
sort of crude (but adequate in this application) electronically
controlled resistance. With Tr2 cut off, Tr1 receives no significant base bias current from Tr2's collector via R1, and it is
therefore cut off and has a very high impedance. This prevents
the unijunction relaxation oscillator from working, and the
output from the chuffer circuit is unmodulated. Thus, with a

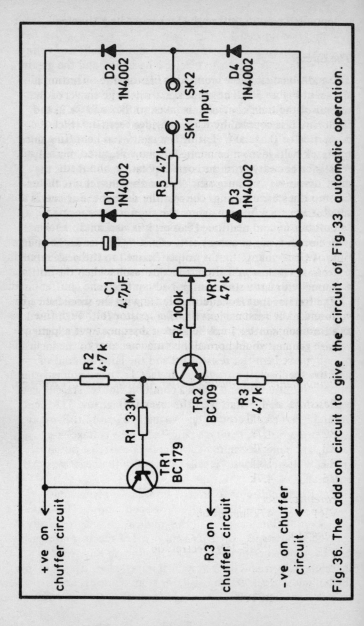

Fig. 36. The add-on circuit to give the circuit of Fig. 33 automatic operation.

88

low track voltage the required unmodulated "hissing" steam sound is produced.

As the track voltage is increased and the collector voltage of Tr2 falls, Tr1 starts to receive a base bias, and the greater the track voltage, the greater the bias on Tr1. This initially causes Tr1 to conduct just sufficiently to give a very low operating frequency from the relaxation oscillator in the chuffer circuit, and then gradually increases the level of conduction so that the operating frequency (and chuffing rate) are brought up to maximum. Thus the required relationship between track voltage and chuffing rate is obtained.

Obviously it is necessary to have the chuffer circuit break from the steady hissing sound to the slow chuffing sound at whatever track voltage causes the train to start moving if a satisfactory and realistic effect is to be obtained. This is achieved in this circuit by first adjusting the train controller for a track voltage that is just sufficient to set the train moving from a stationary position, and then advancing VR1 just far enough to start a slow chuffing action from the chuffer circuit. The start of the train and the chuffing action should then be found to be reasonably well synchronized, although fine adjustments to VR1 can be made subsequently if experience with the unit should prove this to be necessary.

Components: Automatic Chuffer Add-On Circuit (Figure 36)

Resistors, all 1/3 watt 5% (10% over 1M)

R1	3.3M
R2	4.7k
R3	4.7k
R4	100k
R5	4.7k

Potentiometer

| VR1 | 47k lin carbon |

Capacitor

| C1 | 4.7µF 25V electrolytic |

Semiconductors

| Tr1 | BC179 |
| Tr2 | BC109 |

D1 to D4   1N4002

Miscellaneous
0.1in matrix stripboard
Control knob
Input sockets (SK1 and SK2)
Wire, solder, etc.

Construction

It should not be difficult to add the automatic adaptor into the
original chuffer unit, and there is no need for any additional
mounting holes for extra controls since VR1 in the original
circuit is no longer necessary, and can be used as VR1 in the
automatic adaptor circuit. It is necessary to add mounting
holes for SK1 and SK2 on the rear panel of the unit, and these
sockets can be wander types.

The circuit is assembled on a 0.1in pitch stripboard which
has 17 copper strips by 12 holes, and Figure 37 shows the
component layout of this together with the other wiring of
the unit. There are no breaks in the copper strips,
incidentally.

The positive supply for the board is taken from one of the
leads that formerly connected to VR1 in the original chuffer
circuit (the one that connects to the same track as C1 +ve, R1,
etc. on the chuffer board). The other lead which formerly
connected to VR1 of the chuffer circuit now connects to the
add-on unit, and it connects to the same track as Tr1's collector
(see Figure 37). The negative supply for the add-on circuit
is taken from the chuffer circuit board, and the connection can
be made to the hole to the left of the one which takes the
negative lead of C1 in the chuffer circuit (or any other vacant
holes in this row).

Note that S1 of the original chuffer circuit is no longer
required and is disconnected, and it is obviously not necessary
to use a switched potentiometer for VR1 if you are building the
unit in its automatic form right from the start, and are not
building the manual version first. Note also that the single
break in the copper strip of the original chuffer board is not
needed if the automatic version is made, and it should either

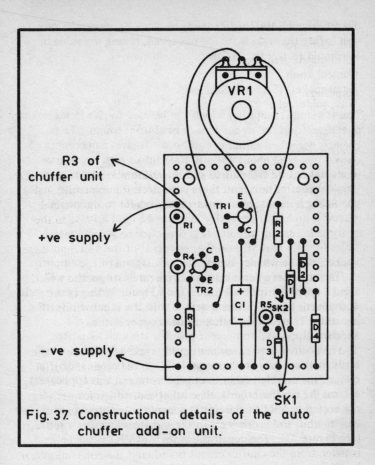

R3 of
chuffer unit

VR1

+ve supply

R1

TR1
E
B
C

R2

R4
C
B
E
TR2

C1
+
−

D2

D1

R5
SK2

D4

R3

−ve supply

D3

SK1

Fig. 37. Constructional details of the auto
chuffer add-on unit.

be left out or bridged with a short piece of wire if it has already
been made.

The component panel is quite small and it should not be too
difficult to find a suitable spot for it in the case of the original
chuffer unit.

It may be possible to optimise the performance of the unit
by altering the value of R1 in the add-on circuit, although this
may well be unnecessary. If the chuffing rate fails to reach
maximum when the train is adjusted for full speed, a
reduction in the value of R1 should cure this problem. If, on

the other hand, the chuffer tends to reach its maximum rate well before the train is set for full speed, raising the value of R1 should recitfy the problem.

Amplifier

This is a simple amplifier which can be used to give loudspeaker operation from the steam whistle or chuffer sound effects projects described earlier in this book. It gives a maximum output power of about 150mW RMS into a high impedance loudspeaker, and this should give adequate volume for most requirements. The circuit is very simple and inexpensive, using just one integrated circuit plus a few discrete components.

The Circuit

Figure 38 shows the complete circuit diagram of the amplifier, and as can be seen from this the circuit is based on the well known LM380N audio device. This IC has inverting (pin 6) and non-inverting (pin 2) inputs, and in this case it is the inverting input that is used. The other input is connected to the negative supply rail to prevent possible stray pick-up here. The LM380N has an internal negative feedback circuit which sets its voltage gain at a nominal level of 50 times (34dB), and this is considerably higher than is necessary in this application. R1 and R2 are therefore used as an attenuator which reduces the voltage gain of the circuit to a level that ensures good results when used with the chuffer and steam whistle circuits. C1 provides DC blocking at the input and VR1 is the volume control.

C3 couples the output signal of IC1 to the loudspeaker and provides DC blocking here. C2 decouples the supply to the preamplifier stage of IC1 and helps to prevent instability due to stray positive feedback through the supply lines. C4 is the main supply decoupling capacitor.

The circuit can be powered from the same source as the sound generator circuit used to provide its input signal, and it will then share the on/off switch of the sound generator circuit. The current consumption of the circuit is typically about 8 to 10mA under low volume and quiescent conditions, but rises to

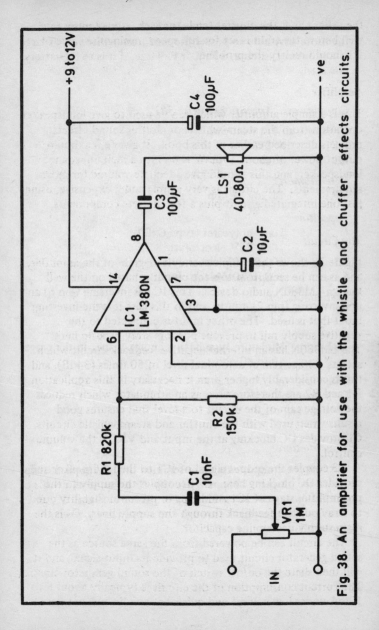

Fig. 38. An amplifier for use with the whistle and chuffer effects circuits.

93

about 2 or three times this level at high volume settings. It is therefore advisable to power the unit from a medium or large 9 volt battery, such as a PP7 or PP9 size, if it is to be battery powered.

Components: Amplifier (Figure 38)

Resistors, all 1/3 watt 5%
R1   820k
R2   150k

Potentiometer
VR1   1M log carbon

Capacitors
C1   10nF polyester (type C280)
C2   10µF 25V electrolytic
C3   100µF 10V electrolytic
C4   100µF 10V electrolytic

Semiconductors
IC1   LM380N

Loudspeaker
LS1   Miniature type having an impedance in the range
            40 to 80 ohms

Miscellaneous
0.1in matrix stripboard
Wire, solder, etc.

Construction

Most of the components are assembled on a 0.1in pitch stripboard measuring 14 copper strips by 19 holes. Full details of the component panel and wiring are given in Figure 39, and this is all quite straight forward and should not give any problems.

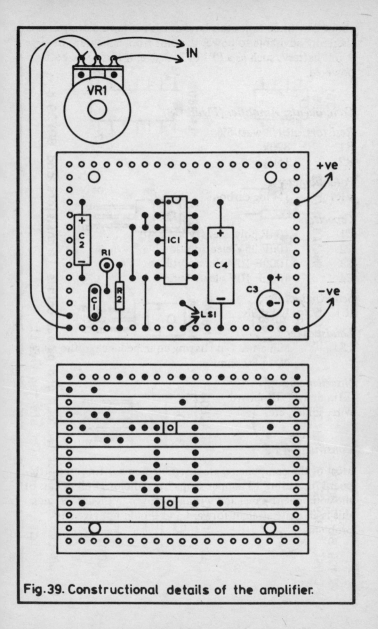

Fig. 39. Constructional details of the amplifier.

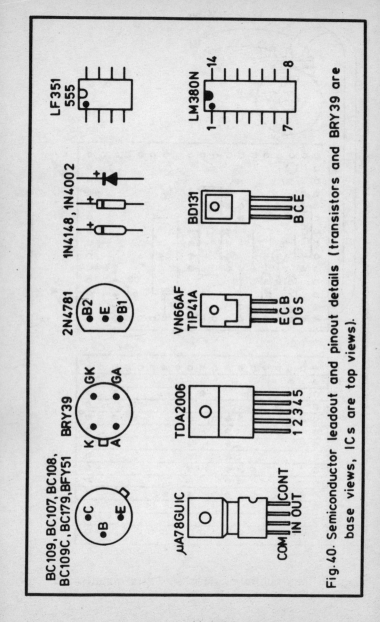

Fig. 40. Semiconductor leadout and pinout details (transistors and BRY39 are base views, ICs are top views).

96

Notes

Notes

Notes

Please note overleaf is a list of other titles that are available in our range of Radio and Electronics Books.

These should be available from all good Booksellers, Radio Component Dealers and Mail Order Companies.

However, should you experience difficulty in obtaining any title in your area, then please write directly to the publisher enclosing payment to cover the cost of the book plus adequate postage.

If you would like a complete catalogue of our entire range of Radio and Electronics Books then please send a Stamped Addressed Envelope to.

BERNARD BABANI (publishing) LTD
THE GRAMPIANS
SHEPHERDS BUSH ROAD
LONDON W6 7NF
ENGLAND

160	Coil Design and Construction Manual	£2.50
205	Hi-Fi Loudspeaker Enclosures	£2.95
208	Practical Stereo & Quadrophony Handbook	£0.75
214	Audio Enthusiast's Handbook	£0.85
219	Solid State Novelty Projects	£0.85
220	Build Your Own Solid State Hi-Fi and Audio Accessories	£0.85
222	Solid State Short Wave Receivers for Beginners	£2.95
225	A Practical Introduction to Digital ICs	£2.50
226	How to Build Advanced Short Wave Receivers	£2.95
227	Beginners Guide to Building Electronic Projects	£1.95
228	Essential Theory for the Electronics Hobbyist	£2.50
BP2	Handbook of Radio, TV, Industrial and Transmitting Tube and Valve Equivalents	£0.60
BP6	Engineer's & Machinist's Reference Tables	£1.25
BP7	Radio & Electronic Colour Codes Data Chart	£0.95
BP27	Chart of Radio, Electronic, Semiconductor and Logic Symbols	£0.95
BP28	Resistor Selection Handbook	£0.60
BP29	Major Solid State Audio Hi-Fi Construction Projects	£0.85
BP33	Electronic Calculator Users Handbook	£1.50
BP36	50 Circuits Using Germanium Silicon and Zener Diodes	£1.50
BP37	50 Projects Using Relays, SCRs and TRIACs	£2.95
BP39	50 (FET) Field Effect Transistor Projects	£2.95
BP42	50 Simple LED Circuits	£1.95
BP44	IC 555 Projects	£2.95
BP45	Projects in Opto-Electronics	£1.95
BP48	Electronic Projects for Beginners	£1.95
BP49	Popular Electronic Projects	£2.50
BP53	Practical Electronics Calculations and Formulae	£3.95
BP54	Your Electronic Calculator & Your Money	£1.35
BP56	Electronic Security Devices	£2.50
BP58	50 Circuits Using 7400 Series IC's	£2.50
BP62	The Simple Electronic Circuit & Components (Elements of Electronics — Book 1)	£3.50
BP63	Alternating Current Theory (Elements of Electronics — Book 2)	£3.50
BP64	Semiconductor Technology (Elements of Electronics — Book 3)	£3.50
BP66	Beginners Guide to Microprocessors and Computing	£1.95
BP68	Choosing and Using Your Hi-Fi	£1.65
BP69	Electronic Games	£1.75
BP70	Transistor Radio Fault-finding Chart	£0.95
BP72	A Microprocessor Primer	£1.75
BP74	Electronic Music Projects	£2.50
BP76	Power Supply Projects	£2.50
BP77	Microprocessing Systems and Circuits (Elements of Electronics — Book 4)	£2.95
BP78	Practical Computer Experiments	£1.75
BP80	Popular Electronic Circuits - Book 1	£2.95
BP84	Digital IC Projects	£1.95
BP85	International Transistor Equivalents Guide	£3.50
BP86	An Introduction to BASIC Programming Techniques	£1.95
BP87	50 Simple LED Circuits — Book 2	£1.35
BP88	How to Use Op-Amps	£2.95
BP89	Communication (Elements of Electronics — Book 5)	£2.95
BP90	Audio Projects	£2.50
BP91	An Introduction to Radio DXing	£1.95
BP92	Electronics Simplified — Crystal Set Construction	£1.75
BP93	Electronic Timer Projects	£1.95
BP94	Electronic Projects for Cars and Boats	£1.95
BP95	Model Railway Projects	£1.95
BP97	IC Projects for Beginners	£1.95
BP98	Popular Electronic Circuits — Book 2	£2.25
BP99	Mini-matrix Board Projects	£2.50
BP101	How to Identify Unmarked ICs	£0.95
BP103	Multi-circuit Board Projects	£1.95
BP104	Electronic Science Projects	£2.95
BP105	Aerial Projects	£1.95
BP106	Modern Op-amp Projects	£1.95
BP107	30 Solderless Breadboard Projects — Book 1	£2.25
BP108	International Diode Equivalents Guide	£2.25
BP109	The Art of Programming the 1K ZX81	£1.95
BP110	How to Get Your Electronic Projects Working	£2.50
BP111	Audio (Elements of Electronics — Book 6)	£3.50
BP112	A Z-80 Workshop Manual	£3.50
BP113	30 Solderless Breadboard Projects — Book 2	£2.25
BP114	The Art of Programming the 16K ZX81	£2.50
BP115	The Pre-computer Book	£1.95
BP117	Practical Electronic Building Blocks — Book 1	£1.95
BP118	Practical Electronic Building Blocks — Book 2	£1.95
BP119	The Art of Programming the ZX Spectrum	£2.50
BP120	Audio Amplifier Fault-finding Chart	£0.95
BP121	How to Design and Make Your Own PCB's	£2.50
BP122	Audio Amplifier Construction	£2.25
BP123	A Practical Introduction to Microprocessors	£2.25
BP124	Easy Add-on Projects for Spectrum, ZX81 & Ace	£2.75
BP125	25 Simple Amateur Band Aerials	£1.95
BP126	BASIC & PASCAL in Parallel	£1.50
BP127	How to Design Electronic Projects	£2.25
BP128	20 Programs for the ZX Spectrum and 16K ZX81	£1.95
BP129	An Introduction to Programming the ORIC-1	£1.95
BP130	Micro Interfacing Circuits — Book 1	£2.25
BP131	Micro Interfacing Circuits — Book 2	£2.75

BP132	25 Simple Shortwave Broadcast Band Aerials	£1.95
BP133	An Introduction to Programming the Dragon 32	£1.95
BP135	Secrets of the Commodore 64	£1.95
BP136	25 Simple Indoor and Window Aerials	£1.75
BP137	BASIC & FORTRAN in Parallel	£1.95
BP138	BASIC & FORTH in Parallel	£1.95
BP139	An Introduction to Programming the BBC Model B Micro	£1.95
BP140	Digital IC Equivalents & Pin Connections	£5.95
BP141	Linear IC Equivalents & Pin Connections	£5.95
BP142	An Introduction to Programming the Acorn Electron	£1.95
BP143	An Introduction to Programming the Atari 600/800XL	£1.95
BP144	Further Practical Electronics Calculations and Formulae	£4.95
BP145	25 Simple Tropical and MW Band Aerials	£1.75
BP146	The Pre-BASIC Book	£2.95
BP147	An Introduction to 6502 Machine Code	£2.50
BP148	Computer Terminology Explained	£1.95
BP149	A Concise Introduction to the Language of BBC BASIC	£1.95
BP152	An Introduction to Z80 Machine Code	£2.75
BP153	An Introduction to Programming the Amstrad CPC464 and 664	£2.50
BP154	An Introduction to MSX BASIC	£2.50
BP156	An Introduction to QL Machine Code	£2.50
BP157	How to Write ZX Spectrum and Spectrum+ Games Programs	£2.50
BP158	An Introduction to Programming the Commodore 16 and Plus 4	£2.50
BP159	How to write Amstrad CPC 464 Games Programs	£2.50
BP161	Into the QL Archive	£2.50
BP162	Counting on QL Abacus	£2.50
BP169	How to Get Your Computer Programs Running	£2.50
BP170	An Introduction to Computer Peripherals	£2.50
BP171	Easy Add-on Projects for Amstrad CPC 464, 664, 6128 and MSX Computers	£3.50
BP173	Computer Music Projects	£2.95
BP174	More Advanced Electronic Music Projects	£2.95
BP175	How to Write Word Game Programs for the Amstrad CPC 464, 664 and 6128	£2.95
BP176	A TV-DXers Handbook	£5.95
BP177	An Introduction to Computer Communications	£2.95
BP179	Electronic Circuits for the Computer Control of Robots	£2.95
BP180	Electronic Circuits for the Computer Control of Model Railways	£2.95
BP181	Getting the Most from Your Printer	£2.95
BP182	MIDI Projects	£2.95
BP183	An Introduction to CP/M	£2.95
BP184	An Introduction to 68000 Assembly Language	£2.95
BP185	Electronic Synthesiser Construction	£2.95
BP186	Walkie-Talkie Projects	£2.95
BP187	A Practical Reference Guide to Word Processing on the Amstrad PCW8256 & PCW8512	£5.95
BP188	Getting Started with BASIC and LOGO on the Amstrad PCWs	£5.95
BP189	Using Your Amstrad CPC Disc Drives	£2.95
BP190	More Advanced Electronic Security Projects	£2.95
BP191	Simple Applications of the Amstrad CPCs for Writers	£2.95
BP192	More Advanced Power Supply Projects	£2.95
BP193	LOGO for Beginners	£2.95
BP194	Modern Opto Device Projects	£2.95
BP195	An Introduction to Satellite Television	£5.95
BP196	BASIC & LOGO in Parallel	£2.95
BP197	An Introduction to the Amstrad PC's	£5.95
BP198	An Introduction to Antenna Theory	£2.95
BP199	An Introduction to BASIC-2 on the Amstrad PC's	£5.95
BP230	An Introduction to GEM	£5.95
BP232	A Concise Introduction to MS-DOS	£2.95
BP233	Electronic Hobbyists Handbook	£4.95
BP234	Transistor Selector Guide	£4.95
BP235	Power Selector Guide	£4.95
BP236	Digital IC Selector Guide-Part 1	£4.95
BP237	Digital IC Selector Guide-Part 2	£4.95
BP238	Linear IC Selector Guide	£4.95
BP239	Getting the Most from Your Multimeter	£2.95
BP240	Remote Control Handbook	£3.95
BP241	An Introduction to 8086 Machine Code	£5.95
BP242	An Introduction to Computer Aided Drawing	£2.95
BP243	BBC BASIC86 on the Amstrad PC's and IBM Compatibles — Book 1: Language	£3.95
BP244	BBC BASIC86 on the Amstrad PC's and IBM Compatibles — Book 2: Graphics & Disc Files	£3.95
BP245	Digital Audio Projects	£2.95
BP246	Musical Applications of the Atari ST's	£4.95
BP247	More Advanced MIDI Projects	£2.95
BP248	Test Equipment Construction	£2.95
BP249	More Advanced Test Equipment Construction	£2.95
BP250	Programming in FORTRAN 77	£4.95
BP251	Computer Hobbyists Handbook	£5.95
BP252	An Introduction to C	£2.95
BP253	Ultra High Power Amplifier Construction	£3.95
BP254	From Atoms to Amperes	£2.95
BP255	International Radio Stations Guide	£4.95
BP256	An Introduction to Loudspeakers and Enclosure Design	£2.95
BP257	An Introduction to Amateur Radio	£2.95
BP258	Learning to Program in C	£4.95